HOW TO SEE
THE BEAUTIES OF

ROME

Practical guide-book with about 200 illustrations in blak
and white and in colour with a monumental plan of the city

BONECHI · EDIZIONI "IL TURISMO„ · FIRENZE
Via dei Rustici, 5

Our augury

Dear Tourist, fellow-countryman or foreigner as you may be, we wish to add our personal greetings to the ritual welcome of monuments, custodians, baedekers more or less serious, and even of hotel keepers. During your stay in the Eternal City may you shed the dull monotonous garment of habit and live all your holiday, long or short as it may be, in another spirit. Remember: this is the ever-beating heart of the world, and it was here that the historic structure of peoples was formed in a splendour of power that has never been equalled, of civilisation that cannot be repeated

Lastly may we add this advice: go to the Fountain of Trevi and throw in your coin. They say this makes Fate grant you a return to Rome. And however often you return you will always seé a Rome that is new and old at the same time, because the City has a thousand faces and a lifetime would not be enough to know them all.

INDEX OF ITINERARIES

4

Ponte Milvio.

SUBJECT INDEX

HISTORICAL NOTE
ON THE CITY OF ROME.

It is not presumption on the part of the compilers of this Guide to condense the history of Rome into a few periods. Many others have done so before, endeavouring to outline the story of the Eternal City more from the point of view of the events of which it was the theatre, than from that of all its monuments, and the traces of universal history that it contains. We will therefore try to give a brief summary of the city's past history, and will ask the reader to forgive us if some important events which are nevertheless of secondary importance in the evolution of this beacon light of civilisation and greatness have been left in the background. We are justified by the fact that this is the task of historians, while we have taken on that of leading the visitor with a sure hand on his essential pilgrimage in the capital of Italy and of Christianity.

Rome began almost by chance when a few farmers and nomadic shepherds stopped to rest on the Palatine Hill in 753 or 754 B. C. for a pause in their nomadic life and in order to take advantage of the mild climate and fertile soil of that and the surrounding hils, to which the Tiber brought the essential contribution of water. There is probably no truth in the tradition whereby these shepherds and farmers lived on the hill of Evandro; this evidently happened during the period when the nomads gave the ground on which they had settled the character of a real settlement and installed the apparatus and collected the belongings relative to an indefinite stay. Naturally the nucleus of the forces that were later to give rise to the existence of Rome was enriched by means of fusion with the natives of different races. It is in fact from intermarriage with Etruscans, Sabines and Latins that a population sprang up which was able to express, in the Latin language and with a Latin spirit, a personality which was soon to become predominant and to absorb the near and distant populations. Opinions differ as to the etymology of the name Rome, it may well have an Etruscan or a Latin derivation. Many interpret the word Rome as meaning « City of the river ».

The city's situation, which was soon shown to be well fortified from a military point of view and strategic from a commercial one, near the sea and on the course of the Tiber as it as, was an important factor in the rapid development of the city which was to become a centre of universal civilisation and well-being. This development was already marked during the period of the « seven kings » although it is not true that the so-called « Servian walls » were erected in this period, or that there were hypothetical political formations or conquests of the type that later made the name of Rome respected and feared throughout the world. It is more probable that there soon arose a very efficient ruling class which particularly in the difficult time of transition from monarchy to republic performed its delicate task to the full and with a stern resolution (510-508) B. C.). This ruling class was at the first prevalently aristocratic and governed through two consuls supported by the wisdom of the senate; but soon the people or plebs obtained the appointment of two tribunes whose first aim was the equalisation of rights between the nobles and the people. Naturally this could not lead to an organisation of the type that is nowadays known as democracy; but a notable

Trajan Forum at the time of Sixtus V. (*XVI century*).

evolution did take place within the ruling classes and the popular assemblies gained in importance with respect to the elected *senate*. The internal movements, instead of injuring the city's growth,
contributed to it, helped to increase commercial exchanges and to
bring about that essential consciousness whereby a people begins to feel
itself really free and sovereign. In the second half of the 4th
century B. C. Rome had acquired unchallenged supremacy over the
whole of Latium, and this happened immediately after the invasion
of the *Gauls*, when the city prepared to face the rude inhabitants of
the mountains (Sannites) conquering them as she was later to con-
quer first the *Etruscans*, then the *Gauls* and the *Greeks* firmly settled
in southern Italy.

This may be considered as one of the first important successes of
Rome in the military field and is largely to be attributed to the fact
that the enemy peoples could not achieve that union and agreement
that, put to a common purpose, would have allowed them to crush
the young population of the City. As early as 270 B.C., little less than
three centuries before Christ, the whole of the Italian peninsula was
already subject to Rome. Military conquest was complemented by
those fundamental elements in life known as culture and civilisation and which are far more essential to a lasting domination than
military victory on the field. Profound transformations began to take

place in the field both of culture and of law, round the splendid « beacon » which had grown up on the banks of the Tiber. Rome, which till then had availed herself of the not inconsiderable efforts of Etruscan civilisation, began to absorb the classical influence of the Greeks who had previously settled in Southern Italy; yet all the while her own, inequivocable spirit developed.

About 250 B.C. Rome began to venture on her first excursions overseas. The two terrible Punic wars which finished in 201 B.C. gave her undisputed sway over the Mediterranean which meant also opening the door to the Near East and the fairly easy conquest of the countries which had avoided the hegemony of Alexander the Great. Meanwhile, in the West, still by the easy way of the Mediterranean Rome soon conquered the populations of Spain and Gaul who had only their rudimental force of arms to oppose. So by means of military victories and constant expansion in the field of law and civilised living, Rome founded the Roman Empire, first as an external dominion, then as an internal organisation. The City on the banks of the Tiber from which military conquest and political and civil ascendency irradiated out became the centre of a world in which law and justice pointed to a future rich in promise.

The Imperial regime true and proper began with Augustus a few years before the vulgar era. While still preserving the form of the republican magistracy, which rested on foundations constituted by the will of the people tempered by the wsdom of the Senate, Rome could not avoid succumbing to an absolutist and monarchist regime, above all as a result of the barbarian pressure brought to bear on the boundaries of the Empire. This meant that Rome as a city began to descend, from that position as beacon light of the world in which her military and civil conquests had placed her. Meanwhile the Emperors no longer lived in Rome, while the plebs were annulled, from a political point of view, from the beginning of the Empire; the Senate itself, which had followed the destiny of the city ever since its origins, was relegated to the position of a mere municipal institution. As a result the troubled decadence of the Empire becomes identified with the decadence of Rome herself, from all points of view, political, demographic, cultural, artistic. The first barbarian occupations take place with Odoacer and Theodoric, but the lowest point of the city's decay is reached during the conflict with the Goths, which lasted twenty years. Although this superficial survey of the history of Rome brings us to this culminating point in the decadence of the Empire and consequently of the City, we must still affirm once more that the City remains unequalled in the world, first and unchallenged in the field of civilisation, of art, and of law, and to her limitless merits must be added the fact of having civilised the most diverse peoples of the Europe and the East. But the destiny of Rome is perpetuated by the fact that a transcendental Will elected the city to be the centre of Cristianity and the seat of the successors of Peter, the Prince of Apostles, whose mortal remains, like those of St. Paul, are still conserved in the city of the Caesars. There can be no doubt that Rome derived greater glory from this particular election since she was transformed from the centre of a military and temporal domination, often subordinated to the force of arms, to the fulcrum of a spiritual force destined to preserve in the world, throughout the centuries, the unchallengable force of brotherhood and human charity.

Piazza San Pietro at the time of Sixtus V. (*XVI century*).

By about 550 A.D. Rome had become a city of the Byzantine empire, secondary in her position even to Ravenna which had become the seat of this empire in Italy. However shortly afterwards the city began to feel the effects of the installation in Italy of the new Franco-Carolingian Empire. In fact Charlemagne was crowned Emperor by the Pope in Rome at the end of the eighth century A.D. Other Emperors were crowned in Rome later. These events gave the city back much of her lost dignity, although Rome became the scene of conflicts between Church and Empire which later culminated in the struggle for the investiture with disputes between the Pope and the Imperial successionists.

Later at the period of the Comunes in Italy other contrasting forces were in conflict in the ancient city: the Papacy and the Empire were opposed in turn by the Roman Comune and the feudal nobility which threatened to reduce the people once more to a sort of bestial slavery. This resulted in the frequent departure from Rome of the various Popes who succeeded one another on the Throne of St. Peter and in a very troubled existence for the Roman Comune, which never reached the heights of strength and splendour of the great Italian Comunes. While on one hand the shorter or longer absence of the Popes resulted in a marked depression in the general tenor of life, it must be recognised that the popular governments enjoyed greater efficiency and continuity. The Pope's definite return had the result, especially in the first decades of the 15th century, of greatly limiting the power of the Comune. However the return of the Papacy to Rome gave back the city its position of artistic and cultural centre among the Italian and European principates.

Unfortunately this golden period was of brief duration, and was ended in 1527 with the so-called *sack of Rome*, which did not however succeed in modifying the terms of the Pope's supreme rule over the city. In fact during the period of the Counter-Reformation, the power of the Pope was reinforced; this epoch coincided with the splendours of Baroque art in Rome. From the political point of view the city had no further aspirations or ambitions, also as a result of the constant neutrality into which it was relegated by Papal policy during the 17th century.

The second restoration began about 1815 under the aegis of Pius VII, and until 1830 the first yeast of patriotism timidly fermented under the clerical regime, so timidly however that it did not succeed in awakening a decided and consistent response to the mounting wave of patriotism which had invaded the whole peninsula. It was not until the time of Pius IX (1846) that Rome became one of the most active and influential centres in the Risorgimento movement. In 1848 the proclamation of the statute and the convocation of Parliament took place. Unfortunately a short time later the spontaneous and therefore excessive bellicism of the supporters of United Italy came into conflict with the moderating influence of the Pope, Pius IX, who was obliged to leave Rome, after the assassination of Pellegrino Rossi and the proclamation of the Roman republic (February 1849) by a Constituent Assembly. Immediately afterwards Giuseppe Mazzini represented the moral vertex of the triumvirate until the French army forced the Roman republic to surrender and restored the Pope for the third time in half a century. However even the French intervention was only an episode shortly afterwards forgotten in the irrepressible desire of the Italians to make Rome Capital of Italy. This happened in September 1870 when Lamarmora's bersaglieri entered Rome by the breach of Porta Pia. And on July 1st 1871 Rome became Capital of Italy in fact.

A « modus vivendi » of peaceful exsestence with Papal Rome was maintained notwithstanding the latent protest of the Vatican, until in February 1929 the final Conciliation between Church and State was establisched by the signature of the Lateran Pact. Meanwhile Italy took part in the bitter conflict of 1915-1918 during which, however, Rome suffered no material damage to her buildings and monuments. This was not the case in the Second World War, during which the Eternal City underwent some bombardment by the Anglo-American forces and the shame of the German occupation immediately after the 8th September 1943. However the city's patrimony of historical and artistic treasures emerged from the war almost intact and it may be said that the greatest number of foreigners who come to Italy now visit the City, owing both to its natural attraction as the capital of Christianity, and to the characteristics and testimonies which have given it the epithet of Moral Centre of the civilised world.

FIRST·ITINERARY

Piazza dei Cinquecento - Piazza della Repubblica - Baths of Diocletian - Santa Maria degli Angeli - The National Museum or delle Terme - Via Nazionale - SS. Apostoli - Piazza Venezia - Palazzo and Museum of Palazzo Venezia - San Marco - Vittoriano.

Piazza dei Cinquecento. — The wide, animated square facing the railroad station Termini is called « dei Cinquecento » (of the 500). The name recalls the 500 heroic Italian soldiers who fell at the Battle of Dogali, in Africa (1887), and the monument erected in the square, in their honour. To the right, are the ruins of the *Agger of Servius Tullius* (378-352 B.C.), built by the Romans as a means of defense, against the invading Gauls.

Piazza della Republica. — The ancient Baths of Diocletian were once on this site. More commonly known as the Piazza dell'Esedra, this square was designed in 1885, by G. Koch. Two porticoed palaces on the perimeter of the square follow the contours of the central exedra (lecture-hall) of the Baths. *The Fountain of the Naiads* is by Guerrieri. Midst the scintillating play of light and water, are a group of bronzes by Mario Rutelli (1901). In the distance are visible the colossal ruins of the Baths of Diocletian.

13

Piazza dell'Esedra: Naiads' Fountain, *by Guerrieri*.

BATHS OF DIOCLETIAN

These were the greatest baths of antiquity and constitute an evidence of the high degree of refinement of the Romans of that period. More than 3,000 bathers could be accommodated at one time in this huge establishment, built by Maximian and Diocletian (298-306 A.D.). Today, we see the Church of Santa Maria degli Angeli, and the Museo Nazionale (or delle Terme) on the site of the ancient ruins.

CHURCH OF SANTA MARIA DEGLI ANGELI

It was built in 1561, by Michelangelo, who transformed one of the great halls of the Baths (the ancient Tepidarium) into the aspect of a church. In 1749, Luigi Van-

SANTA MARIA DEGLI ANGELI. - Interior.

SANTA MARIA DEGLI ANGELI. - To the left: **Tomb of Salvator Rosa**; in the centre: « St. Brunone », by G. A. Houdon; to the right: « St. Jerome », by Girolamo Muziano.

vitelli remodeled the structure. Currently, it is used for official religious ceremonies.

INTERIOR. — Crossing the vestibule (the ancient Calidarium), we enter the church, which at the transept is 91 meters long, 27 meters wide, and 28 meters high. Of the 16 enormous columns, 8, of Egyptian granite, are ancient. In this church, are numerous monuments and tombs of famous people. To the left, the tomb of the Neapolitan poet and painter of the 1600's Salvator Rosa; to the right, the tomb of the painter Carlo Maratta (d. 1713), and one of his most significant works, the Baptism of Christ. In the right corridor to the transept, the statue of St. Brunone by G. Anthony Houdon (1766), about which Pope Clement XIV used to say: « He would speak, if the rules of his Order did not forbid it ». A sundial, on the pavement to the right, is by Francesco Bianchini and Giacomo Maraldi (1702). Noteworthy among the paintings is the « Saint Jerome surrounded by Saints » by Girolamo Muziano, an artist whose works were esteemed by Michelangelo. The tomb of Marshal Armando Diaz (d. 1928) is also to be seen. A fine painting by Domenichino, « The Martyr-dom of Saint Sebastian » is to the right of the main altar, and to the left, « The Punishment of Ananias and Sapphira » by Pomarancio. Behind the main altar, the sepulchre of Pius IV attributed to Michelangelo.

THE NATIONAL MUSEUM OR MUSEUM DELLE TERME

It is to the right of Santa Maria degli Angeli. Inaugurated in 1889, it comprises an important collection of Greek, Roman, and Christian art. At the beginning of this century, the museum was enriched by the gift of the Ludovisi collection.

Upon entering, we come upon the first group of cross-vaulted halls, which grow out of the right wing of the transept of the church. - Hall I: a noteworthy pavement of mosaic; epigraphic fragments; and a sarcophagus with the legend of Phaedra. - Hall II: sarcophagus of the Muses (III cent. A. D.), and a plaster reproduction of the lower part of the Temple of Hadrian (II cent. A. D.). - Hall III: Christian sarcophagi portraying the following themes (in the three sarcophagi at the further end of the room): Moses, and the Water Springing from the Rock; the Arrest of Saint Peter; the Transformation of Water into Wine at the

THE NATIONAL MUSEUM OR DELLE TERME. - To the left: « Dying Gaul and his wife »; in the centre: « The Pugilist »; to the right: « The Discobolus ».

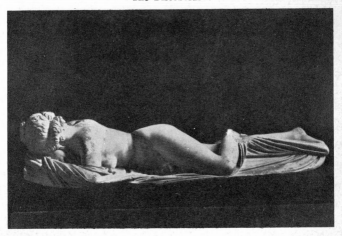

THE NATIONAL MUSEUM OR DELLE TERME. - « Sleeping Hermaphrodite ».

Marriage of Canae; the Multiplication of the Loaves; the Healing of the Blind; the Resurrection of Lazarus. - Hall IV: a fine mosaic on the pavement, portraying the hunting of the crocodiles and hippopotami; an impressive sarcophagus of the combat between the Romans and the barbarians (II cent. A. D.); sarcophagus with Dionysus and Ariadne (II cent. A. D.); monumental statue of Kore, from the original by Alkamenes. - Hall V: Mars and Venus (II cent. A. D.); sarcophagus with Eros and Psyche (III cent. A. D.). - Hall VI: mosaic of a chariot race in the Circus (IV cent.); sarcophagi with scenes of bacchic revelries, barbarians in chains before a Roman general, and the legend of Medea. We exit into the open. - Hall VIII: a collection of rich architectonic marble fragments; to the left, the ruins of the swimming pool or the frigidarium of the Baths. - Hall IX: of an oval form, with two apses; great mosaic of Neptune guiding his chariot of marine horses (II cent. A. D.). - Hall X: reconstruction with original fragments of the sepulchre of Gaius Sulpicius Platorinus, and family (I cent. A. D.). - Hall IX: mosaics. - We come now to a garden with many inscriptions and marbles, and proceed to the main part of the museum. At the left of the entrance-hall is the small *Carthusian Cloister*, site of the famous *Ludovisi Collection*. These works of sculpture were collected by the Cardinal Ludovico Ludovisi, and by Roman princes. The most well-known, and the finest work here is the Dying Gaul and His Wife, a colossal sculpture from Pergamon (III cent. B.C.). Other works include: Hermes Ludovisi, from the V cent. B.C. original; Athena Parthenos, from the original by Phidias; Satyr in the act of Pouring, from the original of the school of Praxiteles; and Orestes and Electra, signed by Menelaos (I cent. B.C.). In the next hall is the *Ludovisi Throne* (the name refers to a throne for the statue of a divinity), a most celebrated work of the V cent. B. C. adorned with fine Greek bas-reliefs. In the archaic style, on the front of the throne, we see the Birth of Venus or Aphrodite. In the same hall, the colossal head of the Juno Ludovisi, in the neo-attic style (I cent. A. D.); a sleeping Erinny, of the Hellenistic period. - Returning to the entrance-hall we enter the *New Galleries*, with noteworthy examples of Greek, Roman and Christian sculpture. - Gallery I: a splendid vase (« rhyton ») in the neo-attic style, and a fine basin of a fountain. - Gallery II: the exquisite nude of the Apollo of the Tevere (V cent. B. C.), the Juno of the Palatine, perhaps the work of Agorakritos, student of Phidias; torso of the Peplos-bearer (« peplophoros »), original Greek of the V cent. B. C.; Aura or Nereid, fragment of a statue of the V cent. B. C.; young Dancer from the V cent. B. C. - Gallery III: here are assembled some veritable masterpieces! The Discus Thrower of Castel Porziano, copy of the original bronze by Myron (V cent. B. C.); Niobide of the Orti Sallustiani original Greek work of

18

the V cent. B.C.; the Venus of Cyrene, discovered at Cyrene, in 1913, original from the IV cent. B.C.; the Efebo of Subiaco, a nude of exquisite grace, Roman copy from the original of the IV cent. B.C.; the Pugilist, an admirable bronze signed by Apollonius, the son of Nestor (I cent. B.C.); the Maiden from Anzio, an original Greek statue of the early Hellenistic period (III cent. B.C.); Young Man leaning on a lance, bronze Hellenistic statue, the Discobolus Lancellotti, faithful copy of Myron's Discus-Thrower. - Gallery IV: Amazon on horseback and a Galatean (III-II cent. B.C.). - Gallery V: decorative marbles of the Roman period. A marble altar and a sepulchral altar with the « dexterarum iunction », of the I cent. A.D. - Gallery VI: solemn statue of Augustus, of a mature age, presiding as a high priest at a sacrifice; head of Nero; head of an Old Woman; bust of the Vestal Maximilla. - Gallery VII: splendid examples of Roman portraiture and the famous ara of Ostia, with decorative themes of Roman legends, from 124 A.D.; head of Vespasian; head of Hadrian; head of a Young Girl. To the right of the door, several bronzes from the famous ships of Nemi. - Gallery VIII: various noteworthy sculptures including a Roman sarcophagus from Acilia (III cent. A.D.); a sarcophagus with pastoral scenes; head of Gallienus. To the right, five smaller galleries with works of sculpture, etc.

On the first floor are two galleries containing mosaics of animal figures, mythological scenes, and of special interest, the mosaic of the four principal factions of the chariots of the Circus. - Returning to the landing, we enter, on the right, the gallery of the *Farnesina stuccos*. These stuccos are from three ceilings of a Roman house of the Augustan period. Thay were found near the Farnesina. Remarkable for their light, fresh quality, they depict landscapes, mythological subjects, and a dancing Victory. In the five walls to the left, *murals of the Farnesina*, found in the same house, in a style intermediate between the second and third Pompeian. Red and black predominate. Of particular interest, in the first gallery, the figures of a Young Man, and of an old Silenus. In the next gallery, Leucothea and Dionysus, Venus and the Graces, in a complex architectural setting. In the paintings of the third gallery, we see elegant meanders against a black background, and a frieze referring to wise king Bocchoris of Egypt. More paintings follow in the subsequent galleries. Returning to the Gallery of the Farnesine Stuccos, and turning to the right, we come to the Gallery of the frescoes of the *Villa Livia at Prima Porta*. A room of the villa has been reconstructed. We see a garden with plants, fountains, animals, environs, etc. all portrayed in a vivid style.

Returning to the ground floor, at the other end of the lobby, we enter the *Great Cloister* attributed to Michelangelo (1565), but, more likely, the work of his pupil, Jacopo del Duca. Of a

perfectly square form, and surrounded by an arcade of one
hundred Doric columns, it is decidedly one of the most beautiful
in Rome .Along the wings of the portico and the garden are
exhibited works of sculpture, and inscriptions. Noteworthy are
the statues of four generals, with relief-ornamented armour.

Via Nazionale. — This is one of the busiest streets of the city.
Many stores are here, and generally it is quite crowded. The first
major intersection, Via Torino, leads to the *Opera House,* and
continuing, to the left, we find the *American Church,* attended by
many members of the American colony in Rome. On the right, we
soon come to the small *Church of San Vitale,* lower than
street-level today, but not in the times of ancient Rome. Built in
V cent., it was reconstructed in 1475. Still further ahead we find
the grand *Exposition Palace,* designed by the architect Piacen-
tini, in 1182, and, still, on the right, a passageway called « Il Tra-
foro Umberto I », that leads into Via del Tritone. On the left is
the beautiful structure of the Bank of Italy designed by the
architect G. Koch, in 1886. At the end of Via Nazionale rises the
Tower delle Milizie built in the 13th cent. in the style of the
Middle Ages. Entering Via IV November, we see to the right
the Via SS. Apostoli, and here we enter the church.

SS. APOSTOLI

The church was erected soon after the establishment
of Christianity, but it was modified many times, and at
the beginning of the 17th cent., it was almost completely
redone by Carlo Fontana. The facade is in the neo -
classic style, and is the work of Giuseppe Valadier (1827),
while the arched Renaissance portico is by Boccaccio
Pontelli, (end of the 15th cent.). It is surmounted by a
loggia with statues of Christ and the Apostles. Under
the portico, to the left, a funerary stele of Giovanni
Volpato by Antonio Canova (1807), and to the right, a
most interesting Imperial eagle, Roman relief work of
the II cent. A. D.

In the baroque interior with naves divided by pilasters, we find
some estimable works of art. The fresco of the Triumph of the
Franciscan Order, on the vault of the central nave is by Baciccia (1707). The Evangelists are by Luigi Fontana. To the left on

the presbitery, the monument to Cardinal Pietro Riario (d. 1474), by Andrea Bregno; Mino da Fiesole (the bas-relief of the Madonna and Child); and Giovanni Dalmata. To the right, above the tomb of Count Giraud d'Ansedun is the tomb of Cardinal Raffaello Riario, condemned in Florence for having participated in the conspiracy againt the Medici. It is by a pupil of Andrea Bregno. - In the confessional crypt, the monument to Raffael della Rovere, of Andrea Bregno (1477). At the end of the left nave, above the door of the sacristy, the beautiful statue of Pope Clement XIV who is imparting the benediction, a masterpiece of Antonio Canova (1787). Worthy of attention, in the vault of the Sacristy is the Ascension, of Sebastian Ricci (1701).

Piazza Venezia. — A major center of Rome, the principal streets converge here. Dominating the square is the majestic *Palazzo Venezia,* and the monument of the *Vittoriano.*

PALAZZO VENEZIA

Constructed betweer 1455-1464, for the Cardinal Pietro Barbo, who later became Pope Paul II. The architect is not known, although the names of Leon Battista Alberti, or Benedetto da Maiano have been suggested. We see a tower, battlemented walls, and the windows of the first floor in the form of a Guelph cross. The two portals that look out on the square, and on Via Plebiscito are attributed to Giovanni Dalmata. Numerous Popes resided here, and in 1494, Charles VIII, the king of France. From the middle of the XVI cent., the ambassadors of Venice lodged here (hence the name), and in 1797 the Austro-Hungarian ambassadors to the Vatican. The Italian government took over the palace, in 1916 and it is now the *Museum of Palazzo Venezia.*

PIAZZA VENEZIA. - Palazzo Venezia.

THE MUSEUM OF PALAZZO VENEZIA

Here are exhibited works of art from many periods.
The first four galleries contain iconographic paintings, Coptic
and Arabian fabrics, ceramics, and a rich collection of armour.
In the V Gallery, the tryptich of Alba Fucense, a relief of the
XIV cent.; Madonna and Child, Romanesque sculpture of the
XII cent.; Crucifixion by Giovanni da Modena; tondo in stucco
from the school of Benedetto da Maiano. In the VI Gallery, a
double Portrait, attributed to Giorgione; a Portrait by Giovanni
Bellini; the Adultress, by Niccolò de' Barbari, and two terracottas
by Jacopo Sansovino of the Miracles of San Marco. In the case,
ivory diptytch of Byzantine art, and the Roman enamel of the
Pantocrator. The VII Gallery is decorated with frescoes of the
'400, with the Labours of Hercules, the work of a Lombard painter: in this gallery, we see paintings by Antonio da Saliba, Callisto Piazza, Bartolomeo Veneto, in addition to tapestries,
enamels and a precious desk of Venetian leather, with the crest
of the Barbo.
We pass now into the halls currently used for exhibitions and

conferences. The Globe Room, with painted colonnades on the walls, by Mantegna; the Concistoro Room; the Regia Room, with simulated architectural decorations attributed to Bramante, and thence to the apartments of Cybo, completed by Lorenzo Cybo, the nephew of Pope Innocent VIII, that comprise Rooms XI to XVII. Here, we see the following paintings: the head of Christ, by Benozzo Gozzoli; the Vision of Saint Bernard, by Francesco Bacchiacca; the impressive Country Feast, by Donato Creti; the Finding of ʾMoses, by Giuseppe Maria Crespi. In addition, a tondo from the workshop of Andrea della Robbia; precious hispano-moorish majolicas; Flemish Tapestries of the XVI cent.; Florentine, Venetian, and Paduan bronzes of the Renaissance, and a beautiful Neapolitan litter-bearer of the first years of the XVIII cent. - In Galleries XVIII-XIX, armour and weapons. Traversing a long corridor, we come to the rooms of the palaz-zetto Venezia. In Galleries XX to XXV, paintings of artists from the XIII-XIV cent.; including Giovanni da Ponte, O. Nelli, Simone da Bologna, and Paolo Veneziano; tapestries with evangelic representations of the XV cent.; Dutch, German, and Russian silver work of the XVII-XVIII cent.; medieval majolicas, ivories, crucifixes, and other objects. - In the following galleries, of particular interest are Russian, Dutch, German and Scandinavian objects of silver; Oriental vases, Beauvais tapestries, fabrics from the cartoons of Francois Boucher; in the cases, a collection of seventeenth century fans, Renaissance rings, necklaces, bracelets, precious objects, an important collection of models in terracotta, and exquisite porcelain statuettes. In addition, paintings by Orazio Borgianni, Guercino, Adam Franz Van der Neulen, Sassoferrato and others.

San Marco. — Turning the corner of the Palazzo Venezia, to the left, we find the Basilica of San Marco. According to tradition, the first church was founded in the IV cent. by Pope Marcus. Restored at the end of the VIII cent. by Pope Adrian I, it was later reconstructed in the IX cent. by Gregory IV, who ordered the mosaics in the apse. Successively, it was reconstructed in the XV cent. by Pope Paul II. Under the portico, attributed to Giuliano da Maiano, a beautiful door and mediaeval marbles. The church has three naves divided by columns. We note on the altar of the last chapel to the right, the painting of Pope San Marco, by Michelozzo da Forlì, and in the apse, mosaics of the IX cent. with Christ in the act of blessing, surrounded by saints, and Gregory IV who is offering a model of the church. In the Sacristy, an interesting tabernacle by Mino da Fiesole.

SAN MARCO. - **Interior.**

Monument to King Victor Emmanuel II (Vittoriano).

Vittoriano. — This monument, dedicated to King Victor Emmanuel II was designed by the Count Giuseppe Sacconi, in the greco-italic style, and was erected 1885-1911. The bronze statue of the King is the work of E. Chiaradia and E. Gallorio. From the magnificent portico of sixteen columns, flanked by propylae, we have a fine view of the city. A flight of stairs, with allegorical groups at the sides leads up to the *Altar of the Nation*, which consists of a statue of Roma, with Procession of Labor to the left, and Love of Country to the right, the work of the sculptor Zanelli. At the base of the statue of Roma, the *Tomb of the Unknown Soldier* of the first World-War.

Altar of the Nation (Statue of Rome).

SECOND ITINERARY

Fori Imperiali (Imperial Forums) - Colosseum or Amphitheatrum Flavium - Arch of Constantine.

Fori Imperiali. — Built in the last days of the Republic, when the Roman Forum became inadequate to accommodate the growing population, these forums added to the magnificence of the city (which was now the Capital of the World). The first was built by Julius Caesar (54-44 B.C.) in the form of a porticoed piazza enclosing religious and non-religious structures, and, in the center, a temple or a basilica, immortalizing the Emperor. Following Caesar, Augustus (32 B.C.); Vespasian (69-75 A.D.); Domitian (97 A.D.); Trajan (113 A.D.), and Hadrian added new forums. During the Middle Ages, and the Renaissance, this monumental area degenerated into a heap of ruins, gradually becoming buried under the soil. With the excavations begun in 1924, fragments of the temples scattered throughout the area came to light.

We begin our visit turning to the left of the monument to Victor Emmanuel II, in Piazza Venezia. Here are two domed churches: *Santa Maria di Loreto* (in the Renaissance style), begun by Giuliano di Sangallo the Younger (1507) the lower portion and finished by Jacopo del Duca (1582) and SS. *Nome di Maria,* of A. Deriset (1738).

Forum of Trajan. — It is below street-level, and is the last (and the most grandiose) of the forums of the Imperial Age. Apollodorus of Damascus designed the vast piazza, and the two libraries, temples, basilicas, and monuments. The ruins of the Basilica Ulpia, for public gatherings, are to be seen, and *Trajan's Column,* built to honour the Victories of Trajan in 113. This is one of the finest monuments of the Imperial Forums. .It is about 30 meters high, and covered with series of spiral reliefs depicting the military exploits of the Emperor against the Dacians in the 1st cent. A. D. The sepulchral vault of the Emperor is under the column. At the summit, is a statue of Saint Peter, placed there by Pope Sixtus V in the XVII cent.

Trajan's Market. — An imposing suite of buildings annexed to Trajan's Forum where the people gathered to exchange views, and to keep up with the news of the day. It too was designed by Apollodorus of Damascus. Here, in the vast semicircle, merchants displayed their goods. On busy days, the market extended as far as the Torre delle Milizie. *The Palace of the Knights of Rhodes* (XV cent.) is on the site now.

Via dei Fori Imperiali. — This street, between the monument to Victor Emmanuel II and Trajan's Forum, connects Piazza Venezia and the Colosseum. Also known as Via dell'Impero, it was constructed in 1932, (on the site of an ancient road) with the aim of showing the monuments of ancient Rome to best advantage. To the right is the Roman Forum, and to the left, are the Imperial Forums. Placed in front of each forum is the bronze statue of the emperor to whom it is dedicated.

Forum of Caesar. — It is to the right of the Via dei Fori Imperiali. It was the earliest of the Imperial Forums, begun in 54 B. C. by Julius Caesar to commemorate the Battle of Pharsalus. The Temple to Venus Genetrix (of which we see 3 beautiful Corinthian columns) was consecrated in 46 B.C. as a tribute by Caesar to the goddess who had led him to victory in this battle. This temple was reconstructed by Trajan in 113 A. D. Among the ruins, we see fragments of a portico of the late Imperial Age, and fragments of the Basilica Argentaria,

Via dei Fori Imperiali.

(added by Trajan) the meeting place for bankers, and
money changers. The bronze statue of Julius Caesar is
a copy: the original may be seen in the Campidoglio.

Forum of Augustus. — We enter from the Piazza del
Grillo, to the left of the Via dei Fori Imperiali. This
forum was built by Augustus (in whose reign Christ
was born), to commemorate the deaths of Brutus and
Cassius (the traitors against Caesar) at the Battle of
Philippi (42 B. C.). We see in the first part, some remains
of the *Temple of Mars Ultor*, the god of war, including
the high podium, and some beautiful, trabeated columns.
To the sides of the temple, the remains of two porticoes,
and two arches of Triumph.

Forum of Nerva. — Constructed in 96 A.D., it was also known as the *Forum Transitorium*, because it served as a passageway between the Forum of Augustus and the Forum of Vespasian. Among the remains, we notice two columns projecting from the enclosing wall, which are fragments of the Temple of Minerva. We also see some ruins of the basement. - With the Forum of Vespasian, of which little remains, we finish our visit to the Imperial Forums, on the left side of the street.

SS. Cosma e Damiano. — The church is to the right of Via dei Fori Imperiali, beyond the entrance to the Roman Forum. Founded by Pope Felix IV in 527 on the site of the Templus Sacrae Urbis, it was restored in the XVII cent. The mosaics of the VI cent. in the apse are especially noteworthy. The vestibule of this church was once the site of the Temple of Romulus.

Basilica of Maxentius and Constantine. — This great building was begun by Maxentius (306-12), and completed by Constantine. It was (as were the Roman basilicas) used as a court of law and an Exchange. Facing the Colosseum, it was 100 meters long, and 76 meters wide, divided in to three naves, with cross vaulting in the central nave, and barrel-vaulting in the others. These magnificent ruins are among the best-preserved, and we can see traces of the original arches and the halls which they enclosed. Every summer, concerts are held here.

Church of Santa Francesca Romana. — Known also as Santa Maria Nova, it was constructed in the second half of the X cent., and many times restored. The last restoration, with the beautiful facade facing the Roman Forum, is the work of C. Lombardi (1615), and the handsome bell-tower, 42 meters high, typically Roman, is of the XII cent. In the interior, with a rich wooden ceiling, we find various works of art, including in the tribune of the apse, beautiful mosaics of the XII cent. of the Madonna Enthroned and Saints.

Temple of Venus and Roma. — It is at the summit of the Via Sacra del Foro Romano, and in antiquity, rose on a great platform, flanked by a double row of columns (fragments of which we can see). The temple was divided into two cells: one dedicated to Venus and the other to Roma. Built by Hadrian, in 135 A.D., it was later restored by Maxentius.

IMPERIAL FORUMS. - Basilica of Maxentius.

COLOSSEUM OR AMPHITHEATRUM FLAVIUM

It is the most important monument of ancient Rome. The construction of the vast building was begun by Vespasian in 72 A. D., on the site of the *Stagnum Neronis* (a lake near Nero's house) annexed to the Domus Aurea, and dedicated by Titus in 80 A. D. It is said that at the dedication of the building 500 ferocious beasts and many gladiators where slain in the arena. The celebration lasted more than three months. In this huge amphitheatre, gladiatorial combats, and venations, the slaying of wild beasts, took place, until 405, when they were abolished by Honorius, the Emperor. Severely damaged by an earthquake in the middle of the V cent. it was converted into a fortress, and during the Middle

Imaginary reconstruction of the Colosseum.

Interior of Colosseum Imaginary Reconstruction.

Above: The outside of the Colosseum; below: Interior of the
Colosseum.

Ages, (because it was covered with marble) served as a rich source of material for the Popes, who used it for the construction of buildings and monuments. What we see today is only a pale reflection of its former splendor. The form is elliptical, with the following dimensions: the major axis of the building, 188 meters, the minor axis 156 meters, the circumference 527 meters. The height of the tiers is 57 meters. Three stories are composed of arches supported by piers, which are pierced with niches In these niches were placed marble statues of divinities, or of important personages. The fourth floor, with windows placed further apart, is decorated with pilasters and corbels. There were four principal entrances directly into the arena and from the arcades, the spectators had access to the multiple tiers of seats. The Amphitheatre, that could cotain more than 50.000 spectators, was composed of a raised platform, and three tiers of seats. The Emperor's box was on the raised platform (or podium) that surrounded the arena, and it could be occupied by no one other than the Emperor. The Senators, government officials, and Vestal Virgins also sat here on separate marble thrones. The first tier of seats was for knights and tribunes; the second for citizens, the third tier and the gallery, for the lower classes. In the arena (which measures 76 by 46 meters) we see today vestiges of the subterranean passages and of the elevators to transport the wild beasts released from their cages. These elevators were operated by hand by the captives. The wooden cross in the center of the arena was placed there by Pope Pius IX to consecrate the area. Ascending a modern stairway, we reach the upper galleries.

ARCH OF CONSTANTINE

Built in 315 by the Senate and the population of Rome to commemorate the Emperor's victory over Maxentius (312), at the bridge of Milvio. Composed of three archways, it is the largest and the best-preserved arch of Rome. Part of the frieze of bas-reliefs adorning this arch do not refer to the deeds of Constantine, but to his predecessors: Trajan, Hadrian, and Marcus Aurelius, these reliefs having been taken from other monuments. The upper reliefs of the arch (facing the Colosseum) represent Marcus Aurelius in his battle with the Dacians; on the opposite side, episode of the battles of Marcus Aurelius, and of Constantine.

Domus Aurea. — It is opposite the Colosseum, in Via Labicana, and is found near the entrance of the Oppius Park, that extends on one of the two Esquiline heights. The Domus Aurea (Nero's Golden House) is the splendid palace that Nero constructed after the disastrous fire of Rome, in 64 A.D. Originally, this palace was composed of many rooms, richly decorated with stucco, and with paintings, which inspired the artists of the Renaissance (the so-calles « grottesche »). Even today, observing the ruins, we can get some idea of its former magnificence. Leaving the Domus Aurea, we ascend a small slope. Here we see part of the ruins of the *Baths of Trajan.*

Temple of Venus and Roma and the Arch of Constantine.

Arch of Constantine.

ROMAN FORUM. - Arch of Titus.

THIRD ITINERARY

Roman Forum - The Palatine.

Panorama of the Roman Forum. — To enjoy a remarkable view of the Roman Forum, we descend from the Piazza del Campidoglio by way of the Via del Campidoglio, to the right of the Senatorial Palace. We come to a terrace, and from here, the Forums of the Caesars, are visible, flanked to the left by the Via dei Fori Imperiali, and to the right by the green Palatine. In the distance is the Colosseum.

Via del Foro Romano. — To the left of the wall of the Roman Forum, are the ruins that have been excavated on the Clivus Capitolinus: the *Portico of the Dii Consentes* (367 A.D.) dedicated to the cult of twelve gods whose images were carved on the backs of the columns; the *Temple of Vespasian* constructed by Domitian in 81 A.D.; the *Temple of Concord* (370 B.C.) commemorating the reconciliation of the patricians and the plebeians. The temple was restored by Tiberius in 10 A.D. Descending the *Clivus Capitolinus*, we reach the *Church of San Giuseppe dei Falegnami* with the subterranean *Carcer Mamertinus*. The prison consists of two chambers. The upper chamber, was the state prison of ancient Rome. Here were imprisoned Vercingetorix, the hero of Gaul, and Jugurtha, king of Numidia. The lower chamber, circular in form, and archaic in construction is said to be the most ancient structure of Rome (300 B.C.). In this room, Saint Peter was imprisoned, and it was here, according to the legend, that a spring burst forth miraculously, enabling Saint Peter to baptize his jailers, Processus and Martinianus. The main entrance of the Roman Forum is on the Via dei Fori Imperiali.

Basilica Aemilia. — To the right of the entrance of the Forum, the Basilica Aemilia, named after Marcus Emilius Lepidus, in 179 B. C. It was destroyed by fire, and by the ravages of barbarians, and now, little remains. It was, together with the Basilica Julia, one of the largest centers in Rome, and was used for the transactions of money-changers and business affairs. In the direction of the Via Sacra, there as a long string of shops.

Curia. — This was the House of the Senate in the Late Empire, founded by Tullus Hostilius. The facade crowned with a tympanum, was preceded by a portico and within was the great meeting-hall, restored by Diocletian, at the beginning of the IV cent. A. D. It was rich with prized marbles. Here are two balustrades called the *Marble Walls of Trajan*, sculptured with reliefs of animals, and episodes from the life of Trajan.

Lapis Niger. — In front of the Curia, protected by roofing, is the famous Lapis Niger, a black marble platform that, according to tradition, covers the tomb of Romulus. Nearby, a fragment of a pyramid, with an archaic inscription which the most ancient example of the Latin language (VI-V cent. B. C.) in existence.

Arch of Septimius Severus. — Built in 203 A. D. to celebrate the decennial of the Emperor's reign. There are three archways. This was one of the most imposing arches of ancient Rome. Over the side arches are reliefs showing episodes of the victorious battles of the Emperor, over the Parthians, and the Arabs of Mesopotamia.

Rostra. — To the left of the Arch of Septimius Severus was the Rostra. This was the tribune of the orators decorated with the beaks of ships captured by the Romans at Antium (338 B. C.). The Rostra was originally in the Comitium and was moved here by Caesar. In front of the Rostra, the *Column of Phocas*, erected in honour of Phocas, the Eastern Emperor (608 A. D.). It was the last monument to be erected on the Forum.

Temple of Saturn. — Built in 497 B. C., it was restored in 42 B. C. We see eight Ionic columns from that late restoration of the III cent. A. D. In the basement of the Temple was the Treasury of the State.

IMPERIAL FORUMS. - Trajan Forum and Column.

The Roman Forum, in the background the Campidoglio.

IMPERIAL FORUMS. - The Forum of Augustus and the Temple of Venus Genetrix.

ROMAN FORUM. - To the left: Temple of Saturn;
to the right: **Basilica Julia.**

ROMAN FORUM. - To the left: **Arch of Septimius Severus;**
in the centre: **Temple of Vespasian;** to the right: **Temple of Saturn.**

ROMAN FORUM. - To the left: **Temple of Castor and Pollux;** in the centre: **Tabularium;** to the right: **Temple of Julius Caesar.**

ROMAN FORUM. - **House of the Vestal Virgins.**

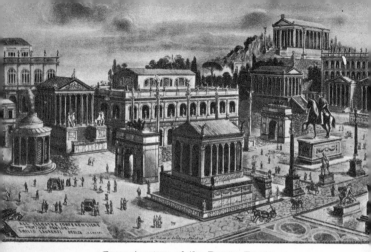

Reconstruction of the Roman Forum.

Reconstruction of the Roman Forum.

The Roman Forum.

ROMAN FORUM. - Arch of Septimius Severus and Temple of Saturn.

Basilica Julia. — Begun by Julius Caesar in ·54 B.C., and completed by Augustus. After a disastrous fire it was restored by Diocletian in 284. Its plan was of a large central hall surrounded by a colonnade of pilasters and a portico. It functioned as a Law Court.

Temple of Castor and Pollux. — It was built in 484 B.C. by the son of Aulus Postiumus to fulfil a vow made by his father before the battle of Lake Regillus. According to legend, the Dioscuri (Castor and Pollux) appeared on the field of battle, and aided the Romans against the Tarquins and the Latins. After the battle, they brought the news to Rome. The three Corinthian columns on the podium, are from the period of the restoration by Hadrian, and by Tiberius. On the left side of the temple, the *Pool of Juturna* (Lacus Iuturnae) where, according to the legend, the Dioscuri when they appeared in the Forum to announce the Victory of Lake Regillus, watered their horses behind the stone basin of the fountain, and an altar sculptured with reliefs, is a chapel to Juturna, from the time of Trajan.

Church of Santa Maria Antiqua. — It is the most important Christian building of the Forum, and one of the oldest churches of Rome (VI cent.). Identified with a pagan structure (perhaps the library of the Temple of Augustus) this was the first temple to be transformed into a Christian Church. In the atrium, we see vestiges of VIII cent. frescoes. The interior has three naves, a narthex and a presbytery with side chapels. On the walls, the remains of VI to VIII cent. frescoes. We are struck by the excellence of the colours and the masterful technique in addition to the harmony of line, and powerful subject matter. Particularly interesting are the frescoes of the left nave with the Story of the Saints; the Adoration of the Cross in the apse, and the Crucifixion in the left chapel (VIII cent.).

Temple of Julius Caesar. — Beyond the temple of Castor and Pollux, and the Pool of Jugurtha, are the ruins of the Arch of Augustus (19 B.C.), and the Temple of Julius Caesar, built by Octavians in 42 B.C. It was on the site of this temple that Caesar's body was cremated.

House of the Vestal Virgins. The home of the Vestals dedicated to maintaining the sacred fire in the near-by *Temple of Vesta.* (This temple was probably built in the first years of the Republic, and subsequently, many times restored. The last restoration may have been in the period of Septimius Severus). A portico of two-stories adorned with statues of the Vestals surrounded an open court that was decorated with flowerbeds, and three cisterns: to the rear, there was a great chapel for images of the gods, and for statues of the emperors. In the court, are pedestals, and the remains of portrait statues.

Regia. — Originally the palace of Numa Pompilius, (according to tradition). Later it became the residence of Pontifex Maximus. Inside there was a sacrarium to Mars, and the Archives.

Temple of Antoninus and Faustina. — Built by Antoninus Pius in honour of his wife, it was inscribed with his own name after his death in 161. In the XI cent. the temple was converted into a church, *San Lorenzo in Miranda.* The baroque facade is from 1602. Ten monolithic columns of cipollino (17 meters high) and an elegant frieze are what remain of the ancient temple.

Temple of Romulus. — We see the bronze door (with the original lock) of the circular temple, which was built by the Emperor Maxentius, who dedicated it to his deified son Romulus. In the VI cent., it was converted into a church and dedicated to *SS. Cosma e Damiano.* The church also included a part of the Temple of Peace.

Arch of Titus. — Erected to commemorate the victories of Vespasian, and Titus who had conquered Jerusalem. On the arch, are bas-reliefs glorifying the Emperor. Among the most famous of these reliefs is the one depicting the soldiers carrying away the spoils from the Temple of Jerusalem. Midst the sacred objects, we see the « seven branched candlestick ». The vault is figured with the Apotheosis of Titus in his triumphal chariot.

THE PALATINE

One of the famous seven hills of Rome, and the residence of the Roman Emperors of the Golden Age. It was here, in 754 B. C. that Romulus is said to have founded the city of Rome. Noble families resided here during the Republic, and Augustus built his palace on this hill when he became Emperor, as did the Emperors of the Imperial period. The Frangipani family converted it into a fortress in the Middle Ages and finally, in the XVI cent. it became the property of the Farnese family, who transformed it into a vast garden. The subsequent archaeological excavations of this area are among the most important in the world.

Orti Farnesiani. — To the left of the Arch of Titus is the Clivus Palatinus that is still paved in the ancient « opus incertum » (so called because the stones are deposited « pell-mell », without a geometrical pattern). Nearby are the Farnese Gardens, once the site of the Palace of Tiberius (later restored by Trajan and Hadrian). From the ruins that remain of this palace, we can form an idea of its former magnificence. The vast garden in the Italian style is a relic of the picturesque Farnese villa of the XVI cent. Here is the *Casino,* with a « nymphaeum ».

Temple of Cybele. — Descending a small staircase we come to a very ancient part of the Palatine, and here, in a little square, we find the Temple of Magna Mater, or Cybele, constructed in

FORO ROMANO

1 - Arco di S●
2 - I Rostri
3 - La Via Sa
4 - Tempio d●
5 - Basilica G

ttimio Severo

cra
Saturno
ulia

6 - Colonna di Foca
7 - Basilica Emilia
8 - Curia
9 - Tempio di Antonio e Faustina
10 - Tempio di Cesare

204 B.C. and later restored by Augustus. What remains is the podium with the enthroned statue of the goddess. In this area are also the so-called ruins of the *House of Romulus* in tufa stone, some steps from the *Stairs of Cacus;* two round cisterns of the V cent. B.C. and remains of huts of the XI cent. B.C.

House of Livia. — This monument, constructed in the last period of the Republic, is among the best preserved of the Palatine. It was thought, at first, to be the house of Livia, the wife of Augustus; but recent studies seem to indicate it was really the house of Augustus. It was, in construction, typically Roman, with rooms opening on a central court, called the « peristylium ». At the front, the three rooms of the « Tablinum » (for state receptions) decorated in the style of Pompey; to the right, the « Triclinium » or dining-room, also decorated with paintings.

Crypto-Porticus. — To the left of the House of Livia, is the passage which leads to the Palace of Tiberius. This passage dates from the time of Nero, and supposedly served to connect the palaces of Augustus and of Tiberius, with the Domus Aurea. From the subterranean passage we climb the stairs to the right, to the Flavian Palace.

The Flavian Palace. — Constructed by Domitian, at the end of the 1st cent. A.D., it was the palace where the Emperors held audiences. The « Domus Flavia » extends, with its archaeological ruins, along the west side of the hill. Behind a portico-like structure at the front, are three hills: to the right the Basilica, where the Emperor held audiences, a hall with parts of the walls, and the apse, and the colonnade still standing; the Aula Regia, richly decorated with columns of pavonazzetto marble, and statues of basalt, traces of which still remain; to the left, the *Lararium,* or personal chapel of the Emperor. From the Aula Regia, we enter the Peristylium where we see fragments of the porticoes, and from here, we enter the splendid imperial *Triclinum,* (banquet-hall) with remains of a marble pavement, flanked by *nymphaeum and fountain.* Beneath the halls of the Flavian Palace are vestiges of the previous structure (1st. cent. B.C.), and beneath the Lararium, an interesting house with paintings, and a mosaic pavement.

Domus Augustana. — Also constructed by Domitian, it was the private residence of the Emperor. It is a two-storied building, facing the valley of the Circus Maximus. The great wall in the form of an exedra was preceded by a file of columns.

THE PALATINE. - Severian buildings.

Stadium. - To the east of the Domus Augustana, this vast area (160 by 80 meters) was surrounded by porticoes and roofless in the central part. One of Domitian's constructions, it is not sure if this arena served for public as well as private functions. On the south side is the hemicycle of the Imperial Tribune.

Baths of Septimius Severus. — To the east of the Stadium are the ruins of the Baths of Septimius Severus. These baths were supplied with water from the « Aqueduct Claudi » (the remains of this aqueduct are to be seen on the Via Appia Antica). Further south, the long terrace of the Place of Severus, commonly called the *Belveder* for the magnificent view of the Circus Maximus, the archaeological area of the Baths of Caracalla, and the distant Alban hills.

The Campidoglio.

FOURTH ITINERARY

Campidoglio - The Senatorial Palace - The Capitoline Museum - Palace of the Conservatori - Santa Maria d'Aracoeli - Theatre of Marcellus - The « Ghetto » - Santa Maria in Cosmedin - Santa Sabina - San Paolo fuori le Mura.

CAMPIDOGLIO

This is one of the classic hills of Rome, and during the first centuries of Roman history, it was an acropolis, and a religious center. The site of the present piazza is between two heights, circa 50 metres high. On one was formerly located the Temple of Juno Moneta (now the Church of Santa Maria d'Aracoeli), and the other, the Temple of Jupiter Capitolinus. There are three ways

51

of ascending the hill : to the left, via the steep stairway that leads to the church; to the right via the winding ramp of Via delle Tre Pile; and from the center, climbing the monumental stairs (« Cordonate », designed by Michelangelo (1536). At the entrance, two Egyptian lions at the sides of the gradient, ornamental gardens. About half way to the top, at the left, a statue of the celebrated Tribune Cola di Rienzo, placed on the spot where he addressed the people after the victorious revolt against the Papacy, in 1354. At the top of the stairs, on the balustrade, the statues of Castor and Pollus, trophies and mile posts.

PIAZZA DEL CAMPIDOGLIO

The harmony of line and proportion of this square, we owe to the genius of Michelangelo, who designed it (1536), after having received the commission of setting up the Campidoglio, on the occasion of Charles V's visit to Rome. It is bounded by three stately palaces: at the further end, the Senatorial Palace; to the right, the Palace of the Conservatori; and to the left, the Capitoline Museum. The majestic bronze equestrian statue of Marcus Aurelius, in the center, is the only one of its kind, no other imperial equestrian statue having ever been discovered (II cent. A. D.).

THE SENATORIAL PALACE

It is on the site of the ancient Roman Senate. Today it is the Town-Hall of Rome. This magnificent Renaissance structure was designed by Giacomo della Porta and

CAMPIDOGLIO. - Bronze equestrian statue of Marcus Aurelius.

CAPITOLINE MUSEUM. - **Dying Gaul.**

CAPITOLINE MUSEUM. - To the left: « **Juno** »; in the centre: « **Cupid and Psyche** »; to the right: « **Venus of the Capitol** ».

54

Girolamo Rainaldi. The double staircase was designed by Michelangelo. The fountain, which is surmounted by a niche with the statue of Roma, is flanked by the statues of the Tiber, and the Nile. Above the palace rises the *Capitoline Tower*, of M. Longhi the Elder (1580). Inside, in the Communal Council hall, is a monumental statue of Julius Caesar, from the Trajan period.

THE CAPITOLINE MUSEUM

Designed by Michelangelo, the beautiful windows, and the portico, are worthy of note. The museum, founded by Sistus IV in the XV cent., was subsequently enriched by additions of Pius V, Benedict XIV, Clement XIII and Pius VI, and comprises the oldest collection of sculpture of the Classic period.

GROUNDFLOOR. — The fountain in the middle of the court is by Giacomo della Porta. The colossal statue of the river, called « Marforio », formed part of the group of « Talking statues » of Rome, with « Pasquin » and « Madonna Lucrezia », who comment-ed on the events, and the misdeeds of the government, and of Roman Personages. - Galleries I-III: document the oriental cults that flowered in Rome in the imperial age. - Galleries IV-V: a series of most important sarcophagi of the museum: the Amendola Sarcophagus, with a scene of combat between the Greeks and the Galateans (II cent. A.D.), and the other, with scenes from the life of Achilles.

FIRST FLOOR. — Approached by a staircase to the right of the lobby. - Gallery I: the celebrated statue of the Dying Gaul, Roman copy of a Greek original from the III cent. B.C., of the school of Pergamon portrays a dying warrior who has fallen in combat. In addition; Cupid and Psyche, from the original Hellenistic statue. Gallery II: the bronze tablet with the inscript-ion conceding the authority to Emperor Vespasian; Laughing Silenus, of red marble, from the original Hellenistic work of the II cent. B.C.; Young boy with a duck, replica of a Hellenistic bronze of the II cent. B.C. - Gallery III: two celebrated Centaurs, in gray marble, from the Villa Hadrian, in the Hellenistic style; wounded Amazon by Cresilas, replica of the original Greek of the V cent. B. C.; the young Hercules, of the Imperial period, and other important works of Sculpture. Gallery IV: 79 busts of eminent personages from the fields of philosophy, the theatre and literature, including Homer, Socrates, Cicero, Epicurus, Lysias, Aeschylus, on the walls, Greek votiv bas-reliefs. Gallery V: 64 busts of Roman Emperors, seated statues of a Roman matron, of the II cent. A. D.; on the walls, Perseus liberating Andromeda, and Silenus and Endymion, high reliefs in the Hellenistic manner. The Gallery is rich in portraits and sculpture. Worthy of note are: the Minerva di Velletri, copy of the original Greek of the V-IV cent. B. C., and the Old Drunken Woman, Pergemon sculpture of the III cent. B.C. - Gallery of the Doves: named after the very fine mosaic of four doves drinking from a basin. It contains a collection of Roman portraits, and a graceful Hellenic statue of a Young girl with a dove. - Cabinet of Venus: here is the world-famous Capitoline Venus, (probably a Roman copy of an original Greek statue of the II cent. B. C.).

PALACE OF THE CONSERVATORI

Also constructed after a design by Michelangelo, it is the site of the Museum of the Conservatori, the New Museum; and the Pinacoteca Capitolina.

COURT. — Here are the ruins of ancient statues including the colossal, marble head of the Emperor Constantine. - Ascending the wide staircase on the landing of which are placed honorary reliefs to Marcus Aurelius, and Hadrian, and the statue of Charles of Anjou, we reach the *Halls of the Conservatori and of Rappresentanza*. In the first hall, of the Horatii and Curiatii, frescoes with legendary episodes of the Regia by the Cavalier d'Arpino, statue of Urban VIII, by Bernini, and a bronze statue of Innocent X by Algardi. - Hall of the « Capitani »: so called for the 5 statues of generals. - Hall of the Triumphs of Marius, with frescoes depicting the victory of Marius over the Cimbri. « Lo spinario » or the statue of a boy picking a thorn from his foot, beautiful bronze sculpture of the I cent. B.C.; the head of L. Junius Brutos, an Etruscan bronze of the IV-III cent. B. C. - Hall of the « Fasti » or of the celebrated Wolf of the Capitol, Etruscan bronze of the VI-V cent. B. C. (the twins were

MUSEUM OF PALAZZO DEI CONSERVATORI. - To the left: « Boy removing a thorn from his foot »; to the right: « St. Sebastian », by Guido Reni.

added in the XV cent. by Pollaiuolo); on the further wall, the Foro-Romano. Hall of the Ducks: bust of Michelangelo in bronze (his death mask); Medusa, marble head by Bernini; statuette of a groom, from the school of Verrocchio. - Passing through the halls that follow, after the ancient Cappella dei Conservatori (Chapel), we come to the *Museum of the Conservatori*. We enter directly into the gallery of the Modern Fasti, where, on the walls, are placed the lists of municipal dignitaries, from 1640 to the present. Turning to the right, we come next to the Hall of the Lamian Gardens, with sculpture from the Esquiline of interest is the « Esquiline Venus », of the I cent. B. C.; the bust of Commodus-Hercules; Girl seated, and other Hellenistic sculpture. We pass to the Hall of the « Magistrati », with statues of public officials of the Constantine period (IV cent. A. D.), and four epigraphs in memory of the honorary citizenship of Rome begueathed upon Petrarch, Michelangelo, Titian, and Bernini. - The Archaic Sculpture halls follow. Here are fragments of ancient sculpture preceding the Empire, works of the Classic period, and replicas of Hellenistic art. Noteworthy is the statue of a young Girl with a peplos, headless; torso of a Youth with right

57

leg raised as if stepping into a chariot, and a Young Girl holding a dove, archaic Greek relief of the 6th cent. B. C. Returning to the gallery, to the left, we enter the Christian halls, where epigraphs of ancient martyrs, or of those persons who were imprisoned by Nero and Caligula are exhibited. - Following the Hall of the Camino, that has a reconstructed litter in the center, and bronzes of the 1st. century, the Hall of the Litter is next, with statuettes of the VII cent. E. C. and Etruscan-Italic ceramics. - Hall of the Castellani, comprising a collection of Greek vases, and the world-famous Aristonothos Crater, the most ancient signed Greek vase, of the VII cent. B. C. - Hall of the Bronzes: interesting is the fiery horse, of the school of Lysippus; a dancing Lari, carrying a vase, and an admirable example of a sepulchral bed. - Hall of the Gardens of Caecenas (Orti Mecenaziani) including the statue of Hercules, of Lysippian inspiration, and a Hellenistic Marsyas. - The seven halls of the new wing follow with an important collection of Roman monuments, portraits, and sarcophagi, among which, most noteworthy is the so-called portrait of Brutos Barbarini, with ancestors, (1st .cent. A. D.).

We enter the garden. Here we see the ruins of the temple of Jupiter Capitolinus, and fragments from the via Flaminia. From here, proceeding to the *New Museum* via the passageway of the Roman Wall, we come next to the remains of the temple of Jupiter Capitolinus begun by Tarquinius Priscus, completed by Tarquinius Superbus, and inaugurated in 509 B.C. - In ten halls, are exhibited funerary urns, archaic sculpture, Polinnia, an admirable Hellenistic work; Pallas, of Castrus Pretorius, of the IV cent. B. C.; Greek art of the V cent. B. C., including the colossal Pallas, replica of the original by Cresilas; torso of Apollo Cithaaroedus; Persephone, in addition to Roman portraits, and sepulchral fragments.

We return to the Gallery of the Fasti Moderni, and ascend the stairs to the first floor, where we find the *Pinacoteca Capitolina*, with works of Italian and other schools, of the XIV-XVII cent. - Room I, School of Ferrara: Annunciation and Sacred Family by Garofalo; Sacred Family by Dosso Dossi. - Room II, Venetian school: Baptism of Christ and a Magdalen, by Domenico Tintoretto; portrait of a Young Man holding a crossbow, by Lorenzo Lotto; Baptism of Christ, a youthful work of Titian; the Adulteress, unfinished work of Palma il Vecchio; Portrait of a Lady by Savoldo two sketches by Veronese, and paintings by Bellini, and others. - Room III: two portraits by Anthony Van Dyck; Romulus and Remus, by Rubens; portrait by Velasquez; Madonna and Child by Luca Cambiaso; Soldier and Witch by Salvator Rosa. - Room IV: Saint Claire and Saint Bartholomew, by Pietro Lorenzetti; Death and the Assumption of the Virgin, by Cola dell'Amatrice. - Room V: Fortune-Telling Gypsy, by

Theatre of Marcellus.

The Temple of Vesta.

Caravaggio; Saint Petronilla, by Guercino; Saint Sebastian, by Guido Reni; Sibyl by Domenichino. -In Rooms VI-VII to the left of Room V, paintings of Domenichino, Carracci, N. Poussin, Reni, Feti. - Room VIII: bronze-gilt Statue of Hercules, found in the Forum, Sacrifice of Polyxena, and Rape of the Sabines, by Pietro da Cortona. - Room IX (Cini Gallery) porcelains; Saint John by Caravaggio; Madonna and Child by Batoni.

CHURCH SANTA MARIA D'ARACOELI

The name derives from the altar erected by Augustus to commemorate the prophecy of the Sibyl which was thought to regard the coming of Christ. It rises on the Capitoline Hill, and was an important center, not only in ancient times, but also in the mediaeval period. Erected in the V cent., in the X cent. it passed to the Benedictines, and in 1250, was transferred to the Franciscans, who reconstructed the church on Romantico-Gothic lines. Above the side door, Madonna and Child and two angels, mosaic of the late XIII cent.

The interior has three naves separated by 22 columns. The rich, gilded ceiling (1575) is adorned with naval symbols, commemorating the victory of Lepanto. To the right of the central door, monument to Cardinal D'Albert, by Andrea Bregno (1485), and on the wall, the tomb of John Crivelli, by Donatello (1432). - The first chapel of the right nave contains (Bufalini Chapel), admirable frescoes by Pintoricchio, with stories of San Bernardino, and the Stigmata of Saint Francis (1485). - Further on, in the center nave, on pilasters, two ambones decorated with mosaics, by Laurentius and Jacobus Cosmas. At the end of the right transept, two Cosmatesque monuments to Honorius IV, and Luca Savelli. - On the Baroque altar of the main chapel, a Byzantine Madonna of the XII cent. - In the center of the left transept, the Chapel dedicated to Saint Helen, with 8 columns, and a magnificent urn of red porphyry. The chapel is supposed to be on the site of the altar erected by Augustus (after the revelation of the Sibyl). The altar is thought to be beneath the pavement. In the left transept the Monument to Cardinal Matteo di Acquasparta, and a fresco of P. Cavallini, Enthroned Ma-

SANTA MARIA D'ARACOELI. - **Interior**

donna and Child with Saints. In the Sacristy, in a chapel to the left, a celebrated Infant Savior, venerated by the people of Rome. In the third chapel of the left nave, Saint Anthony of Padua, by Benozzo Gozzoli (1449 c.).

Via of the Theatre of Marcellus. — This street connects Piazza Venezia with the Aventino. To the left, are the ruins of the Tarpeian Rock, from whence traitors were executed by being hurled to death to the ground. Ahead, to the right, the theatre of Marcellus.

THEATRE OF MARCELLUS

This is the only ancient theatre left in Rome. It was begun by Julius Caeser, finished in 11 B. C. by Augustus, who dedicated it to his nephew Marcellus, the son of his sister Octavia. The first two tiers of arches are in the Doric, and in the Ionic style, and may have been used as a model for the Colosseum. Built upon its ruins is the Palazzo Orsini, designed by Baldassare Peruzzi, in the XVI cent.

THE « GHETTO »
(The Jewish community)

Beyond the theatre of Marcellus, we find the *Porticus of Octavia*, whose origins date from 147 B.C., when Q. Cecilius Metellus (a Roman consul who·had fought in the battles of Macedon) built the porticus to enclose the two temples of Jupiter Stator, and Juno Regina, which had been erected a short time previously. The Porticus was rebuilt by the Emperor Augustus (between 27 and 23 B.C.), and dedicated to his sisters Octavia. All the complex of buildings was called « Opera Octaviae ». Near the Porticus of Octavia, there once stood several other important edifices, which are now completely destroyed, including the Theatre of Balbus (155 B.C.); the Porticus of Phillipus, which was adjacent to the Circus of Flaminius (as was the Porticus of Octavia); the Temple of Apollo; the Porticus of Minucius, and the three temples of the Forum Olitorium, (the vegetable market). The present ruins date from circa 200 A.D., when the buildings were restored by Septimius Severus and by Caracalla. This area is not only of the greatest artistic importance, but, with the passage of time, it has become one of the most interesting quarters of the city. The « Ghetto » or the Jewish quarter in Rome is very ancient. From the first century B.C., there were a certain number of Jews in Rome; and this number grew as the Romans conquered Syria, and Asia Minor. Between 61 and 63 B.C. Pompey deported many prisoners of war to Rome. At first they settled in the Trastevere area, especially along the river, and the Tiberina island. By the early period of the Imperial Age, the Jewish community, well-established, numbered tens of thousands, and after it was recognized by Julius

Synagogue.

SYNAGOGUE. - Interior.

Caesar, it enjoyed all the privileges, and the protection of the Roman Empire. With the advent of Christianity, and with the bitter insurrection in Palestine, the situation of the Jews in Rome changed for the worse. For a long period they were constrained to perform their services clandestinely, and to go into hiding, because between 49-50 A.D., the Emperor Claudius had given the order for their deportation. One false move, on their part, and they would have shared the fate of thousand of prisoners who, after Titus conquered Palestine in 70 A.D. were brought to Rome as slaves, and condemned to the hardest labour (these slaves were employed in the construction of many important monuments, icluding the Colosseum). The exploits of Titus are depicted in a bas-relief on the inner portion of the supporting arch of the Arch of Triumph dedicated to him, and built during the rule of Domitian. It shows the entry of the Roman legions to Rome carrying the rich spoils of the Temple of Jerusalem. This stormy state of affairs lasted until 212 A.D., when the famous edict of Caracalla gave them full Roman citizenship, and legal rights. The center of the spiritual life of the community has always been the Sinagogue. Today, in Rome, there are more than fifteen. In 1961, during the excavations in the archaeological zone of Ostia, the ruins of a Sinagogue of the Roman period came to light. It is the only one discovered till now in Italy and in Europe. Remains of Jewish Catacombs have been found along the Via Appia. One of the largest, and one of the best-preserved, adorned with admirable decoration, is at the Villa Torlonia on the Via Nomentana. Today the Jewish quarter is still thriving, despite the severe trials in the not too distant past, the Nazi persecution, which, on Oct. 16th, 1943, made the narrow lanes surrounding the Porticus of Octavia, a scene of tragedy.

Porticus of Octavia.

Isola Tiberina.

65

PIAZZA BOCCA DELLA VERITA'

The site of the ancient *Forum Boarium,* it is rich in archaeological and medieval monuments. To the right the *House of Crescentius,* built in the X cent. with decorations and ornaments of ancient origin; in addition the *Temple of Fortuna Virilis,* with Ionic columns, built in 100 B. C., an excellent example of italic architecture of the Republican period; to the rear, is the round *Temple of Vesta,* with Corinthian columns, from the beginning of the Imperial Age. - To the extreme left of the square, the *Arch of Janus,* a quadripartite vault with niches intended to receive statues on the two stories, and belonging to the degenerate style of Constantine (IV cent.). Beyond the arch, we see the *Church of San Giorgio in Velabro,* of the VI cent. with portico and bell-tower of the XII cent. and nearby, the *Arch of the Moneychangers* in honour of Sept. Severus and Julia Domna (III cent.), who are portrayed in the act of sacrificing to the gods.

CHURCH OF SANTA MARIA IN COSMEDIN

The word « cosmedin » (ornament) may refer to the embellishments added by Adrian I to the primitive church, when he dedicated it to the Greek exiles in Rome, in the VIII cent. These Greeks had fled to Rome, to escape the persecution in the Orient. Built in the VI cent., on the site of a Roman Temple to Hercules, it had a gynaeceum and three apses. Restored in the XII cent., the bell tower is of that period (Romanesque), and the portico. To the left of the portico is a marble

SANTA MARIA IN COSMEDIN. - To the left: **The Facade**;
to the right: **The Mouth of Truth**.

Arch of Janus.

disk, carved in the form of a triton, from which the name « bocca della verità » is derived. The popular belief was that if a person swore falsely, and would place his hand in the mouth of the mask, it would close upon him.

The internal basilica, in three naves has 18 ancient columns, and various « Cosmatesque » works, (XII-XIII cent.). Or particular interest is the pavement in « opus alexandrinum », the central enclosure of the ancient choir, with ambones of the 11th cent., and a twisted mosaic candelabrum, the canopy over the high altar and an Episcopal Chair in the apse.

Circus Maximus. — To the right of the church, we follow the Via del Circo Massimo, which leads to the Aventine, one of the seven hills of Rome. Ahead, from the piazzale Romulus and Remus, we have a splendid view of the Palatine, the Coelian, the far-away Alban hills, and the Murcia valley, where once extended the Circus Maximus, the most magnificent building in Rome. Founded by Tarquinius Priscus, it was finished in the II cent. B.C., and later enlarged and decorated by Caesar Augustus, Trajan, Caracalla, and finally, by Constantine. It could accommodate 250.000 spectators. In 548, in the time of Totila, the last performances were given.

CHURCH OF SANTA SABINA

On the Aventine Hill, this is the only church in the V cent. Ravenna style, that has come down to us. It was built by Peter, an Illyrian priest, where the house of S. Sabina stood. In the XIII cent. Pope Honorius donated it to Saint Dominic, who built the cloister and enlarged the convent in the atrium, (which corresponds to the ancient facade). To the left, we see a rich door of sculptured wood, with scenes of the Old and the New Testaments in the 18 panels, a masterpiece of early Christian art of the V cent.

The luminous interior has three naves. The Corinthian columns are taken from pagan temples. Over the principal door, fragments

San Paolo.

of ancient mosaics with inscriptions on the blue background of the names of Peter of Illyria, the founder of the church, and Celestine I who consecrated it. The two female figures symbolize the Church of the Gentiles (to the right) and the Church of the Circumcision (to the left). In the central nave, on the pavement, the tomb of Munoz de Zamora, general of the Dominican order (d 1300), and a « schola cantorum » with ambones, reconstructed with ancient fragments (IX cent.). At the altar of the d'Elci Chapel, in the left nave, Virgin of the Rosary, with SS. Dominic and Catherine, by Sassoferrato. - The adjoining convent has a beautiful cloister (1225) where Saint Dominic used to pray.

PORTA SAN PAOLO

This is the ancient Porta Ostiensis, of the Aurelian Wall. The inside portion, with two arches, is from the period of Aurelius (III cent.); the outside, an arch between two battlemented turrets, is from the period of Belisarius (VI cent.). Outside the gate, the celebrated *Pyramid of Caius Cestius,* monument to the Tribune Cestius (d. 12 B.C.), 37 metres high, is covered with slabs of marble.

Crossing the piazzale Ostiense, after several kilometers, we reach the *Ostiense Sepolcreto,* a small Pre-Christian Roman necropolis.

SAN PAOLO FUORI LE MURA

Called also the Basilica Ostiense, it is the largest church in Rome, next to Saint Peter. It was built by Constantine in 314, over the tomb of the Apostle Paul, and enlarged by Valentinian II in 386, and also by Theodosius. It was finally completed by Honorius, his son. The Chancel Arch, decorated with scintillating mosaic, by order of Galla Placidia (V cent.), made this one of the most beautiful churches in Rome. On the 16th of July, 1823, it was almost completely destroyed by a terrible fire. Many of the great works of art were lost. Immediately after, the restoration of the building was begun, according to the original plans, under the direction of the architects P. Belli, P. Bosio, P. Camporesi, and L. Poletti. It was consecrated in 1854 by Pope Pius IX. The entrance is preceded by a quadriportico of 150 columns, designed by Giuseppe Sacconi. In the center, the colossal statue of Saint Paul. On the facade, mosaics of the four prophets, Isaia, Jeremiah, Ezekial, and Daniel. In the middle zone, the mystic Lamb, and in the spandrel, Christ between SS. Peter and Paul. The bronze door with basreliefs, of the central portal, is by Antonio Maraini (1930).

The interior, 120 metres long, has four rows of columns and 5 naves. The columns of the central nave are Corinthian, with

SAN PAOLO. - Interior.

splendid capitals. The ceiling is panelled. On the walls, Medallion
Portraits of the Popes, from Saint Peter to Pius XI. The triumphal
arch of the large nave is decorated with mosaics of the period
of Emperor Honorius and his sister Galla Placidia (V cent.).
We see a representation of Christ, and the Evangelists, and the
24 elders of the Revelation; below, SS. Peter and Paul. At the
sides of the arch, two statues of Apostles. On the High Altar,
the ancient Gothic tabernacle of Arnolfo di Cambio (XIII cent.)
saved from the fire of 1823, a jewel of architecture, sculpture,
and mosaic. In the Confession, beneath the altar, the remains
of Saint Paul. To the right, the beautiful paschal candelabrum,
by L. Vassalletto (XII cent.). The mosaic in the apse dominated
by the great figure of Christ, is the work of artists of the
Republic San Marco (1220). To the left of the apse, the splendid
chapel of Saint Stephan, with the colossal statue of the saint, by
R. Rainaldi, and the Chapel of the Crucifix, by Carlo Maderno,
which contains the Crucifix which is said to have spoken to
Saint Bridget. To the right of the apse, the Chapel of S. Lorenzo, with a triptych of the '400, and a modern choir stall;
the Chapel of Saint Benedict, by Poletti, with 12 Roman columns
from Veio. At the end of the right wing, a rich altar with the

Incoronation of the Virgin, by Giulio Romano, from a design by Raphael. Through the door to the right of the altar, we enter the Hall of the « Martirologio », with frescoes of the XII cent. To the left, is the Baptistry, in the form of a Greek cross, with four ancient columns. From here, we enter the beautiful *Cloister*, with examples of Cosmatesque design, binate columns, elegant frieze, and inscription of mosaic, work of Vassalletto (1193-1214). Around the cloister are fragments of ancient inscriptions and sarcophagi from the Christian era.

SAN PAOLO. - Mosaic in the apse.

SAN PAOLO - To the left: « The tabernacle »; to the right: « Jesus giving a blessing » (Mosaic in the apse).

SAN PAOLO. - The Cloister.

CHIESA DEL GESU'. - To the left: **The Facade**;
to the right: **Altar of St. Ignatius Loyola.**

CHIESA DEL GESU'. - **Statue of Cardinal Bellamarino,**
by Gian Lorenzo Bernini.

FIFTH ITINERARY

Corso Vittorio Emanuele - Church of Gesù - Largo Argentina - Santa Maria Sopra Minerva - Pantheon - Sant'Andrea della Valle - Piazza Navona - Piazza Campo de' Fiori - Palazzo Farnese - Castel Sant'Angelo.

Corso Vittorio Emanuele. — It is the broad street that connects Piazza Venezia with Saint Peter's. Opened circa 1870, it is today the site of many shops, and elegant palaces of the Roman aristocracy.

CHURCH OF GESU'

This church was founded by the Jesuits and belongs to that Order to this day. It was begun in 1568, from the designs of the architect Vignola. The baroque facade was added by Giacomo della Porta, who completed this sumptuous building in 1584.

The interior, in the form of a Latin cross, is single-naved, with side-chapels. Among the many rich decorations, we see in the vault of the nave the breathtaking « Triumph of the Name of Jesus » by G. B. Gaulli, known as « il Baciccia » (1669-83). Il Baciccia was a follower of Bernini. The chapel of Saint Ignatius of Loyola, the founder of the Jesuit Order, is in the left transept. The sepulchre of the Saint is beneath the altar. This altar was said to be the costliest in the world, not only for the great statue of the Saint in solid silver (later melted down by Pius VI to pay a war-debt to Napoleon), but also for the globe of lapis-lazzuli in the Trinity group above the altar. (Today the statue of the Saint is silver-plated). To the sides of the altar, interesting marble statues of allegorical subjects: « The Conversion of Misbelievers to the Faith » by G. Theodon to the left, and « Christianity Triumphing over Heresy » to the right. From the sacristy, we enter the Museum of the Jesuits, which is adjacent to the church.

Largo Argentina. — In the center of this area we see the much-discussed ruins of the *Republican Temples*. These consisted of four temples, of which three were square-shaped, and one circular. Up to now, archaelogists have been unable to identify the cult with which these temples were associated.

We now detour by way of the Via dei Cesari, to the Church of Santa Maria Sopra Minerva. In the piazza della Minerva, we see a small Egyptian obelisk of the VI cent. B. C., on the back of a marble elephant.

CHURCH OF SANTA MARIA SOPRA MINERVA

Built on the ruins of a pagan temple to Minerva, this Gothic church was begun in 1280, by the Dominican brothers Sisto and Ristoro (also the founders of Santa Maria Novella in Florence). The Renaissance facade is by Meo del Caprino (1453).

The interior is divided into three naves, separated by pilasters, with ogival vaulting (the only example in Rome). Here we find many tombs of illustrous personages of the XV-XVI cent. and other valuable works of art. In the V chapel of the right nave, an Annunciation, with gold background, by Antoniazzo Romano (XV cent.); in the VII chapel the tomb of Cardinal De Coca, by Andrea Bregno (1477), and of the Archbishop Sopranzi (1495). In the right transept, the Caraffa Chapel, with a beautiful Renaissance balustrade (1498), and interesting frescoes by Filippino Lippi (1498): the Annunciation, above the altar; the Assumption, on the rear wall; the Triumph of Saint Thomas Aquinas over The Heretics, and Scenes from his Life, on the right wall. The Sibyls on the roof are by Raffaellino del Garbo. Beneath the high-altar, the body of Saint Catherine of Siena, who died in Rome in 1380. To the left of the high-altar, the statue of Christ Carrying the Cross, by Michelangelo (1521). Behind the altar the tombs of Pope Clement VII and Leo X by the Florentine sculptor Baccio Bandinelli. In the left nave, near the altar, the tomb of Beato Angelico (d. 1455). Close to the II chapel is the entrance to the Sacristy, where we find a chapel with frescoes by Antoniazzo Romano, brought here in 1637, from the house where Saint Catherine of Siena died.

The Pantheon.

THE PANTHEON. - Interior.

PANTHEON

It is the most famous, and the best-preserved monument of ancient Rome. First constructed by Agrippa, in 27 B. C., it was restored by Domitian, after the fire of 80, and put together, once again, in its present rotunda shape by Emperor Hadrian. In 609, it was dedicated by Boniface IV as a Christian Church (Santa Maria and Martyres). In the Middle Ages, it served as a fortress. Later times, it was despoiled by the Popes, especially by Urban VIII (Barberini) who melted down the bronze roof for the construction of the baldacchino in Saint Pietro (Bernini), and for 80 cannon of Castel Sant'Angelo. The building consists of a pronaos of 16 columns of red and grey Egyptian granite, 12,50 meters high. Each column is composed of a single block. On the entablature of the 8 columns at the front, we read the dedication to Agrippa. The other columns, arranged in four rows, form three naves.

By way of the marble portal, and the original bronze door, we enter the building, and are immediately struck by the extraordinary harmony of line and proportion and by the sense of space. Above the entablature, runs an attic with niches. Crowning the vast central area, is a marveleus dome (diam. 43,40) divided into square panels. Formerly, these panels were ornamented with gilt bronze rosettes and the seven aediculae along the walls (of alternating rectangular and circular shape) were richly covered with marbles, and adorned with bronze statues, (as were all the niches). In the first chapel to the right, a fresco, the Annunciation, attributed to Antoniazzo Romano. In the second, the Tomb of Victor Emanuel II (d. 1878), and opposite, the Tomb of Umberto I (d. 1900) and Queen Margherita (d. 1926) in the third niche we see the Tomb of Raphael Sanzio. Upon his death in 1520, he had expressed the desire to be buried in the Pantheon. The Madonna is a statue of Baccio da Montelupo.

Palazzo Madama. — Built during the Renaissance, it has been, since 1871, the seat of the Italian Senate. It was named after Margherita of Austria, the wife of Alessandro de' Medici (XVI cent.). The baroque facade is by L. Cardi, and P. Marucelli. It has a great portal with columns, 4 rows of windows, and some splendid bossed work.

SANTA MARIA SOPRA MINERVA. - **Interior.**

SANTA MARIA SOPRA MINERVA. - To the left: **Tomb of Fra Angelico;**
in the centre: « **Christ bearing a cross** », by Michelangelo; to the right:
« **St. Sebastian** », by Tino da Camaino.

CHURCH OF SANT'ANDREA DELLA VALLE

Begun in 1591 by P. Paolo Olivieri, the building was finished in 1650 by Carlo Maderno. C. Rainaldi, in 1663 added the travertine facade, with an imposing portal, a great window, and a series of small lateral balconies, niches, and statues, modifying the plan of Maderno. The dome is one of the most beautiful in Rome.

The interior, a single nave with great side chapels, has a spacious apse, and barrel-vaulting. In the first chapel to the right, a marble statue of Cardinal Giannetti, and on the altar, the Angel who counsels Saint Joseph to flee to Egypt, by Antonio Raggi (1675). In the second chapel, which has been attributed to Giacomo della Porta, a copy in bronze of the Pietà and of Leah and Rachel (from the original by Michelangelo). High up at the end of the nave, the tomb of Pius II (Eneo Silvio Piccolomini, d. 1464), and Pius III (Todeschini Piccolomini, d. 1503), transferred here from Saint Peter's in 1614. The frescoes in the cupola, the

SANT'ANDREA DELLA VALLE. - To the left: **The outside of the church**; to the right: « St. John the Baptist », by Pietro Bernini.

Piazza Navona.

PIAZZA NAVONA. - **Fountain of the Rivers**, by Bernini (detail).

Glory of Paradise, are by Giovanni Lanfranco (1621-25). The four Evangelists, and the angels are by Domenichino. Also by Domenichino are the frescoes on the vault of the apse. The three scenes from the Martyrdom of Saint Andrew are by Mattia Preti (1651).

Palazzo Braschi. — Cosimo Morelli designed this palace in 1780, on the site of the Palazzo Orsini-Santobono, for the nephew of Pius VI (Braschi). It was the last of the princely palaces erected in Rome by the papal families. It is in the form of a trapezoid, with one corner on Piazza San Pantaleo, and another on Via di Pasquino. Here, by the palace, we see the famous « Maestro Pasquino », a fragment of a statue of Menelaus, from the Hellenistic group of the III cent. B. C. portraying Menelaus supporting the dead body of Patrocles. The statue is very famous for the « pasquinades » satirical witticisms) placed on the pedestal by the people, in the period of the Papal State.

Museo di Roma. — This museum in the Palazzo Braschi comprises a collection of painting and sculpture, as well as documents relating to Roman topography, and the customs of the city from the Middle Ages to the present. We ascend the monumental staircase (the work of Morelli - 1805) adorned with sculptures and stuccos, to the first floor, where is traced the historic-topographic development of the city of Rome over the centuries, including documents relating to public and private life. More documents are on the second floor, in addition to a collection of paintings, portraits, mosaics, etc. The *Gallery of Modern Art* is on the third floor, with works of art dating from the 1800's to the present.

THE PIAZZA NAVONA

On this site was the Stadium built by Domitian, hence, the elliptical form of the piazza. In antiquity, it was used for horse-racing, and in the Middle Ages, the Popes would have the piazza flooded and float small boats on the lake for aquatic festivals. The style of Piazza Navona is richly baroque, featuring the works of two great masters: Bernini and Borromini. The *Fountain of Rivers*, by Bernini (1647-51) in the center of the square, represents the four largest rivers of the world: the Nile, the

Ganges, the Danube, and the Rio della Plata. The fountains at the extremes of the piazza are, to the south, the Fountain of the Moor, by Bernini, and the Fountain of Neptune, to the north. The latter dates from 1878.

Church of Sant'Agnese in Agone. — This church on the west side of the piazza is, according to tradition, on the site of the spot where Saint Agnese was publicly exposed before her execution. At this time, by Divine intervention, her long hair became like a veil, covering her from head to foot, and saved her from the gaze of the multitude. Begun by C. Rainaldi, in 1626, it was finished by Borromini (1657) who amalgamated the baroque and the neo-classic styles. To the sides of the domed church are two bell-towers.
The interior is in the form of a Greek cross, rich in the play of light and shadow (chiaroscuro), with great marble sculptures over the altars. The frescoes of the cupola, which is sustained by 8 columns, are by Baciccia.

Palazzo della Cancelleria. — A magnificent example of Early Renaissance architecture, begun in 1483 for Cardinal Riario, the nephew of Sistus IV. The name of the architect is not known. Some see in the long facade, lightly bossed in the lower portions, with arched windows decorated with elegant pilasters, the work of Andrea Bregno, known as « il Montecavallo ». Others see, in the beautiful court with its double portico the elegant style of Bramante, who supposedly finished the palace in 1511. Today it is the residence of the Pontifical Chancellor.

Piazza Campo de' Fiori. — Behind the Palazzo della Cancelleria is the Piazza Campo de' Fiori. It is typically Roman, a lively, food and clothing market, where, every day, the cries of the hawkers blend with the jargon of the people. There was a time when in this square heretics were burned, and criminals hanged. The monument in the center of the square is dedicated to the memory of Giordano Bruno the illustrious philosopher, who was burned alive here in 1600.

PALAZZO FARNESE

The two fountains in the square were created from two enormous granite bathtubs found in the Baths of Caracalla. This magnificent palace, which represents one of

Piazza Navona.

PIAZZA NAVONA. - The Fountain of the Rivers, by Bernini.

the high-points of Renaissance architecture was begun in 1514 by Antonio da Sangallo, the Younger, for the Cardinal Alessandro Farnese (later Pope Pius III). To Sangallo is attributed the facade with its three orders of windows, the vestibule, and the first two stories of the court. Upon his death (1546) the work was continued by Michelangelo who added the big window, the moulding on the facade, the third floor of the court, and the sides. The work was terminated by Giacomo della Porta, who created the other side of the palace, and the beautiful Loggia which is on the side facing Via Giulia.

From the gate we enter the atrium with three naves separated by columns, and thence to the superb court with porticus, closed in two ranges, in the style of the Colosseum. The larger of the two sarcophagi in the court comes from the tomb of Cecilia Metella. On the first floor is the famous Gallery of frescoes depicting mythological subjects, by the painters Carracci, Domenichino, and Reni.

Returning to the Corso Vittorio Emanuele, and continuing in the same direction, on the right side, we come to the Chiesa Nova.

Chiesa Nuova. — Also known as Santa Maria in Vallicella, this church was commissioned by San Filippo Neri. It took thirty years to complete (1575-1605). G. Rughesi (XVII cent.) is the architect of the baroque facade. The interior, of a single nave, was begun by G. Matteo da Città di Castello, and finished by Martino Longhi the Elder. It is rich in marbles and decorations. The roof, the apse, and the cupola are frescoed by Pietro da Cortona. The Virgin in Glory on the high altar, and the two paintings of Saints, on the sides of the presbytery are early works of Rubens (1608). To the left of the apse is the Chapel of San Filippo Neri, beneath the altar of which the Saint lies buried. From the Sacristy, on the vault of which are frescoes by Pietro da Cortona, we enter the rooms in which the Saint once lived.

To the left of the church is the *Oratorio dei Filippini*, one of the best works of Borromini (1637-62), in the dynamic baroque manner. Here, San Filippo Neri composed and presented those choral compositions known as « oratorios ».

Having come to the end of Corso Vittorio Emanuele, we cross the bridge over the Tiber, and turning to the right, we soon come to the Castel Sant'Angelo. In the distance, in the Via della Conciliazione, is the Dome of Saint Peter's.

CASTEL SANT'ANGELO

Also known as the Mausoleum of Hadrian, this huge structure was built by Hadrian for himself and his successors. Begun in 135 A. D., by Decrianus, it was terminated in 139 A. D. by Antonius Pius. Till the time of Septimius Severus (80 years) it was used as a funerary monument, and the ashes of the dead Emperors were placed here. In the form of a circular tower sustained by a square foundation, and crowned by a tree-like tumulus in the form of a cone. On the summit was a bronze chariot with men and horses and a square altar-like structure.

Subsequently the building was used as a fortress; as the residence of princes and popes; as a prison, and as a military barracks. Gregory VII was imprisoned here; Stefano Porcari (1453) was hanged; here the Borgias imprisoned their victims; Cardinal Carafffa was strangled; Giordano Bruno was tried; and the Count Cagliostro imprisoned. The four lateral towers were constructed by Sangallo, under Alessandro VI. Of the original building of the time of Hadrian, only the quadrangular basement of blocks of travertine marble and peporino remains. The building is crowned with Loggia of Julius II. On the summit is the statue of an angel, from whence derives the name. According to the legend, in 590 while Gregory the Great was conducting a procession to avert the terrible plague which was ravishing the city, the Destroying angel appeared to him on the summit of the fortress, sheathing his sword. This was a sign that the plague was over. The statue of the angel commemorates this event. Today this monument is the site of the Museo di Castel Sant'Angelo.

Museo di Castel Sant'Angelo. — We enter through a bronze door that faces the bridge into the *Cortile del Salvatore*. From here we descend to the vestibule, and to the great Roman spiral ramp which leads to the sepulchral chamber. To the left is the staircase which leads to the *Cortile dell'Angelo or delle Palle*, so called because of the marble statue of the angel by Guglielmo della Porta, and the cannon balls of travertine and granite. From here we pass to the old guard rooms, consisting of five halls in which are exhibited a collection of weapons from the Stone Age to the present. To the left of the court are the two *Halls of Clement VIII* with reconstructions of Castel Sant'Angelo and weapons of the XIX-XX cent., and the *Hall of Justice* with various arms. From this same court, we enter the *Hall of Apollo*, with a collection of Renaissance weapons, and the *Chapel of Leo X* with a Madonna by Raffaele da Montelupo above the altar. This hall leads into the *Halls of Clement VII* with rich coffered ceilings of stucco, and a beautiful frieze by Giulio Romano. From here we enter the great *Cortile di Alessandro VI* where we see military curios, models of the Piedmontese and Italian divisions, and Oriental arms from various epochs. Exiting into the small triangular court, a small flight of stairs leads to a little room, (in former times, water was heated hare for the *Bath of Clement VII*), which is rich in stuccos and frescoes of Giulio Romano. Next we come to the *Historic prison-cells*, and to the ancient storerooms. The last small cell is said, to be the cell where Benvenuto Cellini was imprisoned. Returning to the Cortile di Alessandro VI, we climb the stairs to the *Loggia di Paolo III*, built by Antonio da Sangallo, the Younger. From here, to the right, we pass to the semicircular gallery of Alessandro VI, and to the covered gallery of Pius IV. In these rooms are exhibited military costumes, decorations, medals, uniforms of the various duchies, trophies, etc. Having reached the south front of the castle, overlooking Sant'Angelo Bridge, and the *Loggia di Giuilo II*, by Bramante, from here we enter the *Papal Apartment*, that includes the *Sala Paolina*, with beautiful stuccos by Girolamo da Sermoneta, and frescoes of the Roman school of the XVI cent.; the *Room of Perseus*, displaying 15th cent. furniture, a painting by Lorenzo Lotto « Madonna with Saints », a triptych of Zavattari, a statue attributed to Jacopo della Quercia and a precious tapestry. The next room is the *Room of Cupid and Psyche*, with coffered ceiling, furniture of the 1500's, and paintings by Lorenzo Lotto, and B. Montagna. Returning to the Sala Paolina and crossing the narrow corridor, we come to the group of rooms comprising the *Biblioteca* (library), with two large paintings of the 1400's, frescoes by Luzzi, and a large marble fireplace by Raffaello da Montelupo. In the next room, the *Room of Hadrian* (so-called because of a painting of the

Castel Sant'Angelo.

Mausoleum in the frieze) we find a large altar-piece, « Madonna and Saints » by Luca Signorelli, two paintings by Bissolo, and a « Pietà » by Ercole Grandi. In the *Garland Room* are paintings by Antonio Gionima, Dosso Dossi, and N. Poussin. From here a small staircase leads to the *Prison of Cagliostro*, where he was imprisoned in 1789. An expressive « Pietà » by Niccolò dell'Arca is found in the *Cabinet of the Dolphin* as well as « Christ carrying the Cross » by Sebastiano del Piombo, and other paintings. The *Cabinet of the Stork* includes a group of wood carvings of the Veronese school, among which is an admirable « Descent from the Cross ». The *Treasury Room* concludes the series. Here we see a big walnut cupboard and chests where the treasury of the most precious sacred objects, was placed. By way of a small Roman staircase, at the side, we ascend to the *Upper Terrace*. The bronze angel of Verschaffelt was placed there by Benedict XIV in 1753. The view from here is among the most beautiful in Rome.

St. Peter's Square.

SIXTH ITINERARY

Piazza San Pietro - Saint Peter's in Vatican - Vatican Caves - Museums and Galleries of Vatican City.

THE VATICAN CITY

Vatican City rises on the right bank of the Tiber, on the foothills of Monte Mario and Gianicolo. In Roman times, this was the site of the Gardens of Nero, and the Circus, where thousands of Christians were martyred. (Saint Peter met his death here circa 67 A. D.). It is the world center of the Catholic Church. Each year, thousands of Catholics and non-Catholics stream here from all parts of the world. Not only is the Vatican a great spiritual center, but also rich in priceless art treasures of the Renaissance, and of antiquity.

Politically, Vatican City is a completely autonomous small state within the Italian Republic. The « Lateran Pact » of 1929 established its independence. It has its own radio-station, railroad-station, newspaper, and diplomatic representation in the major capitals. Although it has no army, the « Swiss-Guards », who are the guards of the Pope, patrol the gates of the city day and night. The legislative, executive, and judiciary branches of the government are under the full authority of the Pope, and through the medium of the Cardinal Secretary of State, he participates in international affairs. Vatican City has its own stamps, and its own money, which is valid throughout Italy.

PIAZZA SAN PIETRO

From the Via della Conciliazione, where we see the beautiful *Torlonia Palace* to the right, we enter the great, monumental square, Piazza San Pietro, the masterpiece of Bernini, who constructed it between 1656-1667.

PIAZZA OF ST. PETER'S - A Fountain, by Maderno.

SAN PIETRO. - The Facade.

Piazza San Pietro seen from the air.

Via della Conciliazione.

It is oval in form, bound by a semicircular Colonnade, and 240 metres at its greatest diameter. This colonnade is composed of 284 massive columns, and 88 pilasters in travertine marble forming three galleries, 15 metres wide. On the entablature stand 140 statues of saints, and the great crests of Alessandro VII. In the center is an obelisk (25.50 meters high) with four bronze lions at the base, which was brought from Heliopolis, in the reign of Caligula (c. 40 A. D.) and which originally stood in the Circus of Nero. In 1586 Sixtus V commissioned the architect Domenico Fontana to place the Obelisk on its present pedestal. It took four months, with 600 men, and 150 horses. At the top of the shaft is a relic of the Holy Cross. On the pavement below the monument, we see the points of the compass, and the names of the winds. Of the two fine fountains in the square, the one to the right is by Maderno, and the one to the left is from the period of Clement XI (XVIII cent.). Beyond the right colonnade, surrounded by a group of 16th cent. Apostolic Palaces, is the bronze door that leads to the Vatican Palace.

SAINT PETER'S

The largest church in the world, it rises on the site where the Prince of the Apostles, Saint Peter, is buried. In ancient times, many early Christians suffered martyrdom here. Today, it is a Pantheon of Christianity, rich in statues and monuments to the Popes. According to Church tradition, the early Christians erected a small oratory on the site of Saint Peter's Tomb, which was destroyed in 326 when Constantine the Great founded the first Basilica here. It had 5 naves. Over the centuries,

SAN PIETRO. - Interior.

SAN PIETRO. - The Canopy and the bronze Statue of St. Peter.

SAN PIETRO. - The Portico of the Basilica.

the church became lavishly decorated. In 1452 because ruin threatened the building, Nicholas V commissioned Bernardo Rossellino to design a new structure, of more extensive proportions. When the Pope died, in 1455, the work was interrupted. In 1506, Pope Julius II resumed the work on a grand scale. Bramante, under this pope, designed the building in the form of a Greek cross. Bramante did not live to complete the project, and his successors were Raphael, Baldassarre Peruzzi, and finally, Antonio da Sangallo the Younger. Raphael's plan was a Latin cross, but he, too, did not live to complete the work. The project was taken over, in 1546, by Michelangelo, who adopted the design of a Greek cross with a majestic dome. Upon his death, Vignola, Pizzo Ligorio, Giacomo della Porta, and Domenico Fontana continued

PAVLVS·V·PONT·MAX·ANNO·XIIII

LEO·XIII·PONT·MAX

LEO·XIII·PONT·MAX

SAN PIETRO. - The Porta Santa (The Holy Door)

the work. Subsequently, under Paul V, the plan was changed from a Greek to a Latin Cross, by Carlo Maderno, who also designed the facade. The Basilica was dedicated by Urbano VIII, on Nov. 18, 1626.

THE FACADE. — It is 114,69 meters long, and 45.44 meters high, and approached by a grand stairway. The statues of Saint Peter (De Fabris), and Saint Paul (Adamo Tadolini) are at the sides. On the balustrade, sustained by 8 Corinthian columns, and 4 pilasters, stand the colossal statues of the Savior and John the Baptist, in the center; and the Apostles (except Saint Peter) at the sides. (5.70 meters high). There are nine balconies. From the central balcony, the Pope bestows his benediction. Five open entrances lead into the vestibule, (71 meters long; 13.50 meters wide; 20 meters high). Over the central entrance, opposite the main door of the basilica is the great mosaic of the Navicella (St. Peter walking on the sea), designed by Giotto in 1298 and executed by his pupils. This splendid mosaic, used to be in the old Basilica of Constantine. To the left, the statue of Charlemagne, by Cornacchini (XVIII cent.); to the right, Constantine, by Bernini (1670). There are five entrances into the church. The central Bronze door is by Filarete (1445), with reliefs depicting the Lives of Saint Peter, and Saint Paul. The last door on the right is the Porta Santa which is opened every 25 years for the Jubilee.

INTERIOR. — (The dimensions are extraordinary: 15.160 sq. meters in area; 211.50 m. long; the central arm is 186.36 m. long; 27.50 m. wide, 46 m. high; the transept is 137.50 m. long, the cupola from the lantern measures 132.50 m. There are 229 marble columns; 533 of travertine; 16 of bronze; 90 of stucco and 44 altars).

The sense of magnitude we experienced in the monumental Piazza, here, at the threshhold of the church, is even greater. As soon as we enter, we are struck by the solemn, awe inspiring splendor of the cathedral, and by its colossal proportions. Our visit begins with the central nave, which is vaulted, and which corresponds to the portion executed by Carlo Maderno; (commissioned by Paul V) who transformed the basilica into the form of a Latin cross. The disk of red porphyry on the pavement, near the door marks the spot where Charlmagne was crowned Holy Roman Emperor by Leo III, on Christmas day 800 A. D. In the niches of the Pilasters supporting the arches are placed great statues of the founders of religious orders. On the last pilaster to the right, is the bronze statue of Saint Peter, seated on a marble chair, attributed to Arnolfo di Cambio (XIII cent.). From here we proceed to the Cupola of Michelangelo, one of the architectural wonders of all time. It is sustained by four

SAN PIETRO. - Statue of Charlemagne,
by Agostino Cornacchini da Pescia.

SAN PIETRO. - Statue of Constantine, by G. L. Bernini.

colossal piers, round which is the so-called « square corridor » leading to open chapels. The cupola is divided into 16 compartments, and decorated with six rows of mosaics, from a design by Cavalier d'Arpino. Here, everything is on a grand scale: the baroque statues in the niches of the piers are about 5 meters high. They represent Saint Veronica, Saint Andrew and Saint Longinus; the last named is the work of Bernini, who also designed the balconies above the niches. Under the cupola, above the high-altar, rises the famous Baldacchino (or Grand Canopy), of Bernini (1633), commissioned by Urban VIII and made chiefly of bronze taken from the Pantheon. In front of the altar is the magnificent Chapel of the Confession, of Maderno, around which are 95 lamps which burn night and day illuminating the « Tomb of Saint Peter ». In front of the shrine is the statue of Pius VI, kneeling, and praying, by Canova, (1822). We return now to the entrance, and start down the right nave. In the first chapel, at the altar, is the well-known « Pietà » a marble group executed by Michelangelo at the age of 24, in 1500. It is the only work he ever signed. Beside the statue is a spiral column which, according to legend, once stood in the Temple of Solomon at Jerusalem and which Christ leaned against when he disputed with the doctors, (actually, it is a Roman work of the IV cent.). In the vault of the chapel, a fine fresco by Giovanni Lanfranco, the Triumph of the Cross. - Over the entrance of the next Chapel of the Crucifix, by Bernini, is the monument to Leo XII, by Giuseppe De Fabris (1836). Opposite, on the pilaster, is the monument to Christina of Sweden, (who became converted to Catholicism), by Carlo Fontana. In the next Chapel of St. Sebastian, a mosaic copy of the Martyrdom of St. Sebastian, by Domenichino; and the monument to Pius XI, by P. Canonica (1949). Further on, to the right, the Tomb of Innocent XII, with the allegorical figures of Charity, and Justice, and the Mausoleum to the Countess Matilda of Canossa, by Bernini. Next is the Sacrament Chapel, enclosed by a gilt bronze railing, and designed by Borromini. On the altar the great ciborium in bronze, by Bernini, inspired by Bramante's Temple at San Pietro in Montorio, and a fresco of the trinity, by Pietro da Cortona. On the altar to the right, the Ecstasy of St. Francis, a beautiful mosaic copy, by Cristofori, of Domenichin's famous work. Outside of the chapel, to the right, is the statue of Gregory XIII, by Rusconi. In the bas-relief the Pope is surrounded by sages. It commemorates his reform of the calendar. Opposite, the modest tomb of Gregory XIV. - On the right, is the entrance to the Gregorian Chapel, designed by Michelangelo, and executed by Giacomo della Porta .The chapel is rich in marbles, stuccos, and mosaics, in the Venetian style, by Girolamo Muziano« Over the altar, the Madonna del Soccorso, of the XII cent. To the right is the Tomb of Gregory XVI. To the right of the chapel

SAN PIETRO. - The Bronze Door by Filarete.

SAN PIETRO. - The « Pietà », by Michelangelo.

that separates the chapel from the transept, the Tomb of Benedict XIV, by Bracci. On the altar the mosaic, after Subleyras, of the Mass of St. Basil and the swooning of Emperor Valentinus. The transept, to the right was the scene of a great historical event, the famous Oecumenic Council of the Vatican, of 1869-70. It is decorated with three mosaics: to the right, St. Wenceslaus, King of Bohemia; in the center, the Martyrdom of SS. Processus and Martinianus; to the left, the Martryrdom of Saint Erasmus. - In the passage, beyond the curve of the apse, the monument to Clement XIII, the masterpiece of Canova (1784-92). It is pyramidal in form, with two splendid lions at the angles. Over the altar is a mosaic, the Navicella, representing St. Peter walking on the waves, after Lanfranco. We see next, the Chapel of St. Michael and the mosaic of St. Michael the Archangel, after Guido Reni. The most beautiful mosaic of the basilica, is the Saint Petronilla ,after Guercino. - In the passage to the apse, to the right, is the Tomb of Clement X; to the left is the fine mosaic of St. Peter resuscitating Tabitha, after Placido Costanzi. - We come now to the tribune, where, in a blaze of golden light, rise four colossal statues of bronze (5 meters high) representing the Fathers of the Church: Saint Ambrose; Saint Augustin, Saint Athanasius, and Saint John Chrysostom, supporting the Chair of Saint Peter, (by Bernini - 1656). The bronze chair is said to enclose the wooden seat of the Apostle. Above, the dove of the Holy Ghost, in a glory of angels and clouds. To the right of the Chair, the beautiful monument to Urban VIII, by Bernini; to the left, the monument to the Farnese Pope Paul III, by Guglielmo della Porta. In the passage which follows, the funeral monument to Alexander VIII, by De Rossi. To the left, a mosaic of Saint Peter curing a paralytic, after a painting by F. Mancini. - We enter next the Chapel of the Madonna della Colonna: to the right is the Tomb and the altar dedicated to Saint Leo the Great, with a splendid high-relief, by Algardi (1646). The Pope is in the act of stopping Attila, while the Apostles Peter and Paul look on threateningly. To the side, the so-called Madonna della Colonna, (because the image is painted on a marble column of the old basilica). In the short passage to the left transept, the Tomb of Alexander VII, by Bernini, and his pupils. On the altar, the Sacred Heart of Jesus, a modern mosaic from a design by Muccioli. - Left transept: above the three altars of the left transept, the following fine mosaics: to the right, the Incredulity of St. Thomas, after Camuccini; in the center, the Crucifixion of St. Peter, after Guido Reni; to the left, SS. Martial and Valeria, after Spadarino. In the next passage, to the left, is the mosaic called « The Lie », because it represents the punishment suffered by Ananias, for having lied to Saint Peter. The original design was by Pomarancio. Opposite, the mausoleum of Pius

SAN PIETRO. - Monument to Innocent XII, by Filippo Valle.

VIII, by Pietro Tenerani. The door beneath the monument leads to the *Sacristy* and to the *Treasure of Saint Peters*. Crossing the vestibule adorned with columns, we come to the central hall, the octagonal Sagrestia Comune. On the left opens the Sagrestia dei Canonici. The Madonna, is by Giulio Romano. Above the altar, the Virgin with SS. Peter and Paul, is by F. Penni. Returning to the Sagrestia Comune, we enter next the Sagrestia dei Beneficiati, where, in the small chapel, stands the celebrated ciborium, with two angels, by Donatello, and the venerated Madonna della Febbre, attributed to Lippo Memmi. From here, we may visit the Treasury of the basilica, which features a collection of church ornaments preserved over the centuries. In the glass cases are many precious relics, church vestments, etc. Of special interest are: The Cross of Bisanzio Giustino (VI cent.); the dalmatic, said to be of Charlemagne (XI cent.); two candelabra of Pollaiuolo; the Codex of San Giorgio in Velabro with miniatures of the XIV cent.; candelabra attributed to Cellini; and the platinum chalice donated to Pius VI by Charles III. Returning to the basilica, we enter the Cappella Clementina, of Giacomo della Porta. Over the altar is a mosaic representing a Miracle of St. Gregory, (when the white cloth of the chalice became stained with blood). To the left, the neoclassic Tomb of Pius VII, by Thorwaldsen. The mosaics of the cupola, and the walls portray scenes of the Old Testament, and of the Doctors of the Church. They are after the originals by Pomarancio. Before proceeding to the left nave, we observe, at the left pillar, the Altar of the Transfiguration, a beautiful mosaic, from the original masterpiece of Raphael. - In the passage, to the right, the monument to Leo XII, who was Pope only 15 days; to the left, the Tomb of Innocent XI, after Maratta. - To the right, is the very rich Cappella del Coro, in which the Daily Services are held. The decorations in stucco are by Giacomo della Porta. In the passage which follows, to the left, is the famous bronze tomb of Innocent VIII, by Antonio del Pollaiuolo (1498). The funeral monument appears above the tomb. To the right, the monument to Pius X, by Astorri. - The next Chapel of the Presentation, features « The Presentation of the Virgin », a mosaic after Romanelli. On the wall, to the left, the monument to Benedict XV. - To the right of the next passage, the monument to Maria Clementina Sobiesky, wife of the Pretender James Stuart III, by the architect F. Barigioni. Opposite, the monument to the Stuarts, (who are buried in the grotte), an impressive work by Antonio Canova (1821). The chapel which follows is the Baptistery, The font once formed the cover of a sarcophagus in which the Emperor Otho II (983) was buried. The gilt bronze cover is by Fontana. The mosaic, on the central hall, of the Baptism of Christ in the Jordan, is after Maratta; to the right, the Baptism

SAN PIETRO. - Statue of St. Peter.

SAN PIETRO. - **Interior of the Cupola.**

SAN PIETRO. - The Confession.

of the Centurion, after Procaccini; to the left, the Baptism of SS. Processus and Martinianus, after Passeri.

THE ASCENT TO THE CUPOLA. — We enter from the left nave. It is possible to go to the top either by climbing 537 stairs, or by using the elevator, which takes us to the gallery under the roof of the basilica, where stand the statues of the Apostles, and from where we may proceed on foot to the very summit. It is from this angle that we can appreciate the cupola, in all its magnificence. On this gallery, are the quarters of the « sanpie-trini », the workmen charged with the maintenance of the cupola. We come next to the first railing which is 53 meters high. Next via a narrow, spiral staircase to another flight and the second railing, 73 meters high, and finally, by way of a stairway, which requires a bit of agility, we ascend to the balcony which is 120 meters high. From here, the view is stupendous. The Ball of the Cupola (diam. 2.50 m.), which can hold 16 people at a time, is reached by ascending a nearly vertical ladder.

Grotte Vaticane. — The entrance to the « Vatican Caves » is to the left of the basilica, beyond the arch of the Bells, where the Swiss Guards and the Pontifical Gendarmes are posted; along the perimeter of the massive wall constructed by Michelangelo. The grottos were dug out of the stratum between the floor of the actual cathedral, and the previous Basilica of Constantine. In fact the present church is more than 30 meters above sea level, while the original basilica was little more than 27. In this layer, master architects of the Renaissance excavated the Sagre Grotte Vaticane, or Crypt. We enter, the first group of niches, by way of a narrow passage. Here are exhibited fragments of inscriptions, mosaic compositions (IV-XVI cent.), tombstones (XIV-XV cent.), sarcophagi, and in the first hall to the left, the splendid mausoleum of Sixtus IV, a very fine bronze monument by Antonio del Pollaiuolo (1484). Continuing, we descend a steep staircase, to the right, to the Lower Grottos. (For this visit we need a special permit). Here are the pagan and the Christian necropoli, of the II-III cent., and here, as recent excavations of ten years duration would seem to indicate, was buried Saint Peter. Entering the spacious Grotte Vecchie, that correspond to the crypt of ancient Basilica of Constantine, we find it to be divided in three naves separated by massive pilasters that support the floor of the church above. Along the walls are numerous tombs of popes, and altars adorned with mosaics and sculptures of the XV cent. Outstanding are the tombs of Boniface VIII, Nicholas III, Emperor Otho II, Gretory V, and that of Carola, Queen of Cyprus. To the right is an interesting mosaic of the Savior between

SS. Peter and Paul; the latter is touching Peter's shoulder, re-legating authority to him. Nearby, in the central nave, the beautiful statue of Saint Peter. At the altars on the central wall, in the center, is the Majesty; to the right, the Madonna between SS. Peter and Paul; to the left, the Pietà. At either side of the altars is a doorway which leads to the Grotte Nuove, or the New Crypt, which extend around the Confession, with vaults frescoed in the grottesque style, walls adorned with marble statues in niches, and precious bas-reliefs. Here we may see the Tomb of Pius II, by Mino da Fiesole, and Giuseppe Dalmata (c. 1471). Returning to the entrance, and entering the corridor opposite to the one we took previously, in the hall to the left, is the great sarcophagus of Junius Bassus, Prefect of Rome (d. 359): the most beautiful example of Early Christian sculpture of the IV cent.

MUSEUMS AND GALLERIES OF VATICAN CITY

To reach the museums of Sculpture, (including the Egyptian Museum, and the Etruscan Museum) and the Pinacoteca, the galleries of painting, we follow the right colonnade of Piazza San Pietro a little more than a third of the way. From here, we may see the wall of the corridor which connects the Vatican with Castel Sant'Angelo. Through a door in the wall of Leo IV, we proceed down the Via Porta Angelica, Here, to the left, opposite the crossing of Borgo Pio, is the gate of Sant'Anna, one of the entrances to Vatican City. We continue, however, along the Vatican Walls, and turn to the left at the Piazza del Risorgimento. Always following the Walls, and walking down the Via Leone IV, we turn once more to the left, at the Viale Vaticano. Here, close by, is the monumental entrance to the museums. By, ascending the spiral stairway to the portico, we may enter the Pinacoteca Vaticana, to the right or, by way of the atrium of the Quattro Cancelli (Four Gates), to the left, the vestibule of the Ancient Museums.

PINACOTECA VATICANA

This is a very rich collection of paintings, comprising masterpieces of many periods, and many styles, from the primitives to the moderns.
Room I: Paintings of the Byzantine school and of the Primitives. St. Francis of Assisi, one of the few signed works of

VATICAN GALLERY. - « The Transfiguration », by Raphael.

VATICAN GALLERY. - « The Deposition », by Caravaggio.

Margheritone d'Arezzo (1216-93); Madonna with Child by Vitale da Bologna; Judgement Day, of the Roman school of the XV cent. - Room II: Paintings of Giotto, and of the school of Giotto: Stefaneschi triptych, by Giotto, by Cardinal Stefaneschi, painted on both sides, and revealing the pictorial qualities of Giotto, the great innovator of Italian painting (which up to that time had been Byzantine in style); the Stories of St. Stephen, and a St. John the Baptist, by Bernardo Daddi; a Blessing Christ, by Simone Martini; Christ in front of Pilate, by Pietro Lorenzetti.

Room III: the so-called Beato Angelico Room, because of his important works here: the Miracles of S. Nicholas of Bari, in bright colors, and with a beautiful luminous quality; and the Madonna and Child, suffused with a sense of mystical grace. In the same room, the Incredulity of St. Thomas, by Benozzo Gozzoli; the Death of the Virgin; and a Crucifixion, by Masolino da Panicale. - Room IV: works of Melozzo da Forlì: Sixtus IV, and the humanist Platina. Also paintings by Marco Palmezzano. Room V: dedicated to artists of 1400' s: Pietà, by L. Cranach the Elder; Miracle of St. Vincent Ferrer, by Ercole dei Roberti; Pietà, by Giovanni Bellini. - Room VI: containing a polyptych collection: outstanding are the ones by Crivelli (XV cent.) of the school of Le Marche, the Madonna with Child, Saints, and Crucifixion; Antonio Vivarini Saint Anthony, abbot, and other Saints: Nicola di Liberatore, the Inconronation of Mary. - Room VII: with works by Perugino: Enhroned Madonna with Child, and Saints, the Resurrection, Saint Flavia and Saint Placido Also, the Incoronation of the Madonna, by Pintoricchio, and pupils.

Room VIII: works by Raphael; the Incoronation of the Virgin (1503); the Madonna di Foligno (1512), a composition rich in harmony and elegance a predella with the Theological Virtues; and the Transfiguration, the last work of the master, who finished the upper portion only. (It was completed by Giulio Romano). Here too are the 10 famous Brussels Tapestries, with episodes from the Acts of the Apostoles, woven from cartoons by Raphael, the work of Pieter van Ae|sten (1516). - Room IX: sketch of Saint Jerome, by Leonardo da Vinci, and a moving composition of Giovanni Bellini, the Burial of Christ (Pietà). - Room X: the Titian Room, so-called because of the famous Madonna dei Frari, painted by the artist in his maturity. Also, paintings by Veronese, Sebastiano del Piombo, Giulio Romano, Paris Bordone, Fra Bartolomeo, and others.

Room XI: works of Girolamo Muziano, Barocci, Vasari, Carracci and Cola dell'Amatrice. - Room XII: the famous Deposition from the Cross, the masterpiece of Caravaggio, in which a shaft of light envelops the figures, emphasizing their plastic qua|ities; the Communion of St. Jerome, by Domenichino. Also, works

VATICAN GALLERY. - « The Redeemer », by Giotto.

VATICAN GALLERY. - « Scene from the life of San Nicola »,
by Beato Angelico.

VATICAN GALLERY. - « Scene from the life of San Nicola »,
by Beato Angelico

VATICAN GALLERY. - « The Coronation of the Virgin »,
by Pintoricchio.

by Guido Reni, Guercino, N. Poussin, and others. - Room XIII: works by Maratta, Ribera, Crespi, Murillo, Luca Giordano e Pietro da Cortona. - Room XIV: paintings of various subjects, including Astronomical Obeservations, by Donato Cresti; the Triumph of Mars, by Rubens; the Hunters, by Philip Roos. - Room XVI: a series of portraits including the famous Portrait of Doge Nicolò Marcello, by Titian; the Portrait of Gregory XII, by Girolamo Muziano, the Portrait of George IV of England, by T. Lawrence.

Having seen the Pinacoteca, we return to the Atrium of the Four Gates, which |eads to the Cortille della Pigna, with a vast apse, by Bramante. To the left, we ascend to the Sculpture Museum.

PIUS CLEMENTINE MUSEUM

The name derives from the two founders. Pius VI and Celment XIV.

We begin our visit in the *Greek Cross Hall* which contains mosaics and sarcophagi of the II - III - IV cent. Outstanding among these are: The porphyry sarcophagus of St. Helen, the mother of Constantine, with high-reliefs (IV cent.); porphyry sarcophagus of Constantina, the daughter of Constantine (IV cent.); sarcophagus, found at Torpignattara (IV cent.). - *The Round Hall*: on the floor, we see the magnificent mosaic in color, representing the Battle between the Greeks and the Centaurs (I cent. A. D.). Great statues and busts are placed in the niches along the wall. Noteworthy are: the colossal statue in gilded bronze of Hercules, (I cent. A.D.); statues of a Goddess, from the origina| Greek of the V cent. B.C.; Juno Sospita, of the II cent. A.D.; the bust of Jupiter, found 'at Orticoli, a Roman copy of an original Greek work of the IV cent. B.C. - *Hall of the Muses* contains statues of the Muses, the patrons of the arts, whose divine help has been invoked by many poets throughout the ages. A statue of Apollo is also to be found here. In addition, busts of the Roman period, portraying illustrius Greeks, such as Epicurus, Socrates, Homer, Plato, Aristotele, Euripides. - *Hall of the Animals*: admirable is the statue of Meleager with his dog, and the head of a wild-boar who has just been killed, from the original by Scopas (IV cent. B.C.) - *Hall of the Statues*: outstanding here is Apollo Saurocthonous, where the young god is portrayed leaning against a tree-stump, a Roman copy of an original Greek bronze by Praxiteles, (IV cent. B.C.); Eros of Centocelle, a replica of the ori-

VATICAN GALLERY. - « St. Jerome », by Leonardo da Vinci.

VATICAN GALLERY. - « Madonna and Child with Saints Dominic and Catherine », by Beato Angelico.

PIUS CLEMENTINE MUSEUM. - Laocoon.

ginal Greek of the IV cent. B.C.; bust of Triton, from the original Hellenistic work of the II cent. B.C.; Penelope, from the original Greek of the V cent. B.C.; Sleeping Ariadne, from the original Hellenistic work of the III-II cent B.C. - *Hall of the Busts* divided by arches into four sections. It contains statues of divinities, and the portraits of illustrious Romans. Noteworthy is the bust of Octavian as a youth (31 B.C. - 14 A.D.); Caracalla (211-217 A.D.); Trajan (98-117 A.D.) - Returning to the Hall of the Statues, we pass next to the *Cabinet of the Masks*, so-called for the beautiful mosaics forming the floor found at the Villa Hadrian, at Tivoli (II cent. A.D.). This square hall with Oriental alabaster columns, has frescoes with mythological themes on the ceiling. Of the statues of gods and nymphs, of particular interest is the Venus of Cnidos, a copy of the famous statue by Praxiteles (IV cent. B.C.); Venus at her bath, a careful copy of the original of Diodalses of Bithinia; the three Graces, Roman sculpture inspired by a Hellenistic original; to the side of the entrance, a funerary stele, from the original Greek of the V cent. B.C. - We return to the Hall of the Animals, and from here we proceed to the *Octagonal Court* which is the old court of the Belvedere. In four divisions surrouding the court, are placed some of the most important, and the most beautiful statues in the history of Western art. To the right, the *Cabinet of the Laocoön*, from the celebrated group of the I cent. B.C., found in 1506, in the vicinity of the Baths of Titus on the Esquiline. The statue portrays the revenge of the gods on a Trojan priest, Lacoön, who had invoked the wrath of the gods by warning his countrymen not to admit the Trojan horse within the walls of the city. In revenge, the gods sent two enormous serpents out to the sea, to destroy Laocoön and his two sons. The *Cabinet of Apollo*, with the Apollo Belvedere a replica of the Greek god of light and beauty, from the bronze original by Leochares (IV cent. B.C.). In the Cabinet of Canova is the celebrated work Perseus and two boxers, Creugas and Damoxenus of classic inspiration. In the *Cabinet of Antinous* is the statue of Hermes (Mercury) erroneously thought to be Antinous, a copy of an original of the school of Praxiteles.

Crossing the court we enter the *Round Vestibule*, a circular hall with a handsome basin of pavonazzetto marble. To the left is the *Cabinet of Apoxyomenos*, with the statue of the athlete who is scraping himself after the contest, a Roman copy of an original bronze by Lysippus (c. 330 B.C.). - To the right is the *Atrium of the Torso* exhibiting the celebrated Belvedere Torso, the work of Apollonius of Athens, in the late Hellenistic period (I cent. B.C.). This magnificent fragment was much esteemed and studied by Michelangelo. From the atrium we descend the stairs to the Museo Chiaramonti.

CHIARAMONTI MUSEUM

It is composed of the Chiaramonti Galleries, founded by Pope Pius VII, whose family name was Chiaramonti; of the Lapidary Galleries (for which a special permit is necessary), which include a collection of 5000 pagan and Christian inscriptions; the New Wing and other rooms containing parts of the collections of the Pius Clementine Museum.

CHIARAMONTI GALLERY. — It is arranged in a long corridor divided by pilasters into 60 compartments. Among the numerous monuments we see: a Roman Sarcophagus of the II cent. A.D. with reliefs depicting the myth of Alcestis; the bust of Efesto, Roman copy from the original Greek work of Alcamenes (V cent. B.C.); Hygeia, the goddess of Health, copy from the original Greek of the IV cent. A.D.; Ganymede with the Eagel, from the bronze original of Leochares (IV cent. B.C.), and a colossal head of Augustus.

THE `BRACCIO NUOVO. — (The New Wing). This luminous hall, adorned with marbles and ancient columns, was constructed by Pius VII. Among the famous statues, we see: Silenus nursing the infant Bacchus, from the oriignal of the IV cent. B.C. by Lysippus; the statue of Augustus of Prima Porta (where it was found), one of the finest likenesses of the Emperor, dressed in magnificent armour; the bust of Ceasar, which is in the apse; Statue of Demosthenes, copy of the original bronze by Polyeuktos, erected by the Athenians in 280 B.C.; Wounded Amazon, a replica of the Amazon by Polycletus; the statue of the Nile, a majestic work, copy from the original of the Alexandria school, of the II cent. B.C.; the 16 boys represent the 16 cubits of the annual rise of the Nile as recorded by Philistratus. Here too is a copy of Doryphorus, from the famous original by Polycletus.

Leaving the New Wing, we return to the vestibule of the Pius-Clementine Museum, and from here, we ascend a flight of stairs to the *Hall of the Racing Chariot*. Under the dome, built during the time of Pius VI, we see a magnificent Roman chariot in marble of the 1st. cent. A.D., reassembled by the sculptor, Franzoni (1788). In the hall are several fine Roman copies of famous Greek works, including the so-called Sardanapalus, Roman copy of a bearded Dionysus, from the original of the IV cent., B.C.; statue of a Roman wearing a toga, from the I cent. B.C.; the Discobolus, from the original by Myron (V

CHIARAMONTI MUSEUM. - The Nile.

cent. B.C.); replica of the Discobolus of Naucide (V-IV cent. B.C.). Leaving this gallery, we enter next, to the right, the *Gallery of the Candelabra*, divided into 6 sections, with columns, and copies of rich Roman candelabra. Here too are ancient statues of the gods, of idols, of warriors, including some copies of original archaic and Hellenistic works. We now retrace our steps till we come to a flight of stairs which we descend. On the landing, to the right, is the Etruscan Museum.

Etruscan Museum. — It was founded in 1837, under Gregory XVI. Composed of nine halls, it contains the objects excavated in the southern part of Etruria, from 1828-1836. It also contains material from subsequent excavations in Lazio, at a later period. Hall I: funerary stele; architectural fragments, four sarcophagi (V-I cent. B.C.). - Hall II: precious objects from the world-famous Regolini-Galassi tomb, an Etruscan tomb from Cerveteri (VII cent. B.C. which was found to be almost intact); other tombs from the same necropoli. - Hall III: an important collection of bronzes, gold-objects, glass, candelabra, necklaces, rings, etc. Most noteworthys the Mars from Todi, a great loricated (covered with defensive plates) statue of the

IV cent. B.C. - Hall IV: an admirable collection of terra-cottas, and funerary urns of various periods. The Guglielmi Hall: here are exhibited collections of objects from the necropoli of Vulci, donated to the museum by the marchese Guglielmi, in 1937. - We return now to Hall I, and enter Hall V-VIII, in which are exhibited a precious collection of Greek, Etruscan and Italic vases, found in Etruscan tombs. Especially important (Hall VI) is a large Amphora by the Painter Exekias showing Achilles and Aiax (VI cent. B.C.) playing dice, and the Crater from Vulci, considered one of the most beautiful Greek vases in existence (Hall VII).

Hall of the Assyrian reliefs: here are a series of cuneiform inscriptions, pertaining to the Assyrian Kings from the IX to the III cent. B.C. - We return to the entrance of the Sculpture Museums, and we enter the Egyptian Museum.

The Egyptian Museum.
— This museum also was instituted under the pontificate of Gregory XVI (1839). It is composed of ten halls, and contains a valuable documentary of the art and the civilization of ancient Egypt. Hall: 1: Hall of the Sarcophagi because of the three great sarcophagi, in black basalt, of the VI cent. B.C. (Saitic period) which are found here. On the walls are paintings in red granite above which is a blue and starry sky. - Hall II: here we see reproduction of portraits of famous personalities of the Egyptian world. Outstanding is King Mentuhotep IV, who lived during the XI dunasty (XXI cent. B.C.); the statue of the goddess Sachme (V cent. B.C.); a throne for the statue of Rameses II (the statue has been lost); a colossal granite statue of Queen Tewe (XII cent. B.C.) and other sculptures. - Hall III: here are exhibited works of the artists of the Roman period (II-III A.D.) who were inspired by Egyptian art. These works were found at Hadrian's Villa at Tivoli, and the Iseo of Campo Marzio, the Temple dedicated to Egyptian cults. Hall IV: various statuettes, among which we see a basalt Naoforos (priest holding a little temple), the only Egyptian monument that refers to the conquest of Egypt by Persian King Cambysius (525 B.C.) - Hall V: a collection of wooden mummy cases and funerary steles; outstanding is the one pertaining to Iri, a dignitary of the IV dynasty. - Hall VI: monuments relating to the cults, and mummies of animals. - Hall VII: here we see exhibited the linen that enveloped the mummy of Queen Nefertari, the wife of Rameses II; linens, vases, necklaces, and other objects buried in tombs. In the glass-case, a collection of scarabs that where placed on the chests of the mummy. Halls VIII-IX: contains a collection of papyri in hieroglyphic on hieratic characters (this is the « running » form of hieroglyphic). - Hall X: the Grassi Collection.

 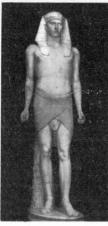 

EGYPTIAN MUSEUM. - To the left: « Queen Tue »; in the centre: « Antinous »; to the right: « Naoforo Udjeharresnet ».

Here we see Egyptian, Hellenistic and Arabic objects, found in Alexandria in Egypt, and donated to the museum in 1953. - We return to the atrium of the Four Gates. Opposite, is the entrance to the Library.

LIBRARY OF THE VATICAN

It was formed through the diligent efforts of many Popes, who, since the beginnings of Christianity, dedicated themselves to the collection of documents and incunabula. The true founder of the library was Nicholas V (1450). In 1588, Sixtus V commissioned Domenico Fontana to construct the splendid halls. Today the library contains 500.000 volumes, 60.000 ancient manuscripts, and 7.000 incunabuli.

The Library is composed of several compartments: the first section is the *Museo Profano* (in contradistinction the Museo Cristiano) of the Library. In the cabinets we see a fine collection of small Greek, Roman and Etruscan bronzes, ivories, mosaics, etc. from various collections or excavations; The next hall is the *Galleria Clementina*, with frescoes depicting the life of Pius VII; the *Alessandrina Hall*, added by Paul V with frescoes on the wall depicting scenes from his life. From here we enter the Sistina Hall, constructed by Domenico Fontana, of two naves and with frescoes of the Roman school of the XVI cent. In the glass cases, we see precious manuscripts, including the Codex Vaticanus B. or early 4th cent. Bible, in Greek; the Virgil Palatino (V cent.); the Roman Virgil (V cent.); the celebrated palimpsest with the « De Republica » of Cicero (IV cent.); Breviary of Mattias Corvinus, written in 1497; Botticelli's illustrations of the Divine Comedy; autographs of Petrarch, including the « Rime ». The next two halls in this section are adorned with fine frescoes. The next *Galleria of Urbano VIII* contains an exhibit of astronomical instruments of the XVI cent. From here, we enter the Museo Sacro (Christian museum), founded in 1756, by Benedetto XIV and containing the treasure of the « Sancta Sanctorum ». In Hall I-II-III, are conserved Early Christian utensils, chiefly from the Catacombs (including glass vessels, lamps, ivories, gems, and other objects in gold and bronze); tools, and objects in metal, enamel, ivory etc. From Hall III, we enter the *Hall, of the Nozze Aldobrandine*, named after the celebrated mural « Nozze Aldobrandine » (because it was purchased of Card. Aldobrandini by Pius VII), one of the most beautiful and precious specimens of ancient wall decoration, of the Augustan Age. It represents the Marriage of Peleus and Thetis. At the further end of the Hall III is the Chapel of Pius V, with frescoes of the life of St. Peter Martyr, from designs of Vasari. In Hall IV, are exhibited holy canonicals. - In Halls V-VI (which are generally closed) we see relics of the treasure « Sancta Sanctorum ». Returning to Hall IV, we cross a little room, and enter the « Appartamento Borgia ».

APPARTAMENTO BORGIA (BORGIA APARTMENT)

These rooms are named after Pope Alexander VI Borgia, who lived here, and ordered the decoration. (He commissioned the most famous artists of the times for this work, including Pintoricchio (492-95). The ornamentation is rich and lavish, according with the taste of this pope.

Hall I: « of the Sibyls », named after the 12 lunettes of the ceiling where we see figures of Sibyls and Prophets, in fresco, of the school of Pintoricchio. - Hall II: « The Credo », after the Prophets and the Apostles portrayed alternately in the lunettes, and discoursing on the Apostle's Creed, which is written on scrolls. It is by Pier Mattia d'Amelia, a follower of Pintoricchio. - Hall III: « Of Science and Liberal Arts ». Containing allegories of the seven Liberal Arts in each of the lunettes, it is mostly the work of Antonio da Viterbo, « Il Pastura ». - Hall IV: « Of the Saints ». This is a masterpiece by Pintoricchio who decorated it lavishly. On the ceiling we see the myths of Isis and Osiris; Io and the bull Api. In the lunettes, proceeding from the entrance to the right, the Visitation of the Virgin; SS. Anthony and Paul in the desert; the Discourse between Saint Catherine of Alexandria and the philosophers; the story of Saint Barbara, of the Chaste Susanna, of the Martyrdom of Saint Sebastian. Over the door, a tondo of the Madonna and Child surrounded by Angels, also by Pintoricchio. - Hall V: « Of the Mystery of the Faith ». Here we see representations of the mysteries of the life of Jesus, and of Mary. The decorations are attributed to Pintoricchio. In the lunette, to the right, the Resurrection (the portrait of Alexander VI in pontifical robes may be observed in the lower portion, to the left), the Epiphany, the Nativity, the Annunciation, the Ascension, Pentecost, the Assumption. - Hall VI: « Of the Popes ». The ceilings here are decorated with stuccos and frescoes, by Perin del Vaga, and Giovanni da Udine (XVI cent.) and six tapestries of the Flemish school of the XVI cent.

THE SISTINE CHAPEL

This celebrated private chapel of the Popes is where the solemn ceremonies of the Holy See take place, and the conclaves for the election of the Popes. 40.50 meters long, 13.20 meters wide, and 20.70 meters high, it was constructed in 1473-84, under Sixtus IV. The Sistine Chapel is considered one of the most sublime masterpieces in the history of world-art. The great Michelangelo can be appreciated here, in all the grandeur and majesty of his genius. In addition, some of the most illustious artists of the Italian Renaissance worked in other parts of the hall. The white marble screen dividing the Singing Gallery from the Chapel is the work of Mino da Fiesole, Giovanni d'Almata and Andrea Bregno.

THE SIDE WALLS. — The 12 frescoes (6 on each side) of the lateral walls are by various Tuscan and Umbrian painters of 1481-83. To the left, we see important episodes from the life of Moses, and, to the right, episodes from the life of Christ. On the left wall, starting from the altar: 1) the Journey of Moses into Egypt, and Circumcision, by Pintoricchio; 2) Moses and the Daughters of Jethro, by Botticelli; 3) the Crossing of the Red Sea, by Cosimo Rosselli; 4) Moses delivering the Commandments on Mt. Sinai, by Cosimo Rosselli; 5) Punishment of Korah (in the background, the Arch of Constantine), by Botticelli; 6) the Death of Moses, by Luca Signorelli. - On the right wall from the altar: 1) the Baptism of Christ, by Pintoricchio; 2) Temptation of Our Lord, by Botticelli; 3) the Calling of Peter and Andrew, by Ghirlandaio; 4) Healing of the Lepers, and the Sermon on the Mount, by Cosimo Rosselli, and Piero di Cosimo; 5) St. Peter receiving the Keys, by Perugino; 6) the Last Supper, by Cosimo Rosselli. In the niches, between the windows, portraits of Popes, by Domenico Ghirlandaio, Cosimo Rosselli, Botticelli and others.

THE CEILING. — It is decorated with the famous frescoes of Michelangelo, commissioned by Julius II. Michelangelo considered himself a sculptor and not a painter, therefore, when the order came from Julius II to decorate the Sistine Chapel, he did all he could to get out of it, but to no avail. The entreaties of Julius II finally won over the reluctant artist, who began the work in 1508. It lasted 4 years, the physical effort involved was considerable. The artist worked for 4 years, on a scaffolding, with his head continually thrown back. The frescoes are of Biblical themes, and include figures of Prophets and Sibyls. The treatment is highly plastic and three-dimensional; a sculptural, rather than a pictorial approach, and this is especially evident in the modelling of the figures. On the central portion of the ceiling are nine subjects, in alternately small and large oblong compartments, with scenes of the Old Testament. In the large triangular compartments at the springing of the vault, are sitting figures of the prophets and sibyls. Among the many great works, is the Creation. God comes near to Adam, who is lying inert, and with a simple touch of his hand imparts the magic spark of life. Commencing from the side near the altar, the subjects are in the following order: 1) Separation of Light and Darkness.

The Sistine Chapel, by Michelangelo.

SISTINE CHAPEL. - To the left: « **The Delphic Sibyl** »;
to the right: « **The Prophet Jonah** », by Michelangelo.

SISTINE CHAPEL. - To the left: « **The Prophet Zaccharias** »;
to the right: « **The Eritrean Sibyl** », by Michelangelo.

SISTINE CHAPEL. - « The Last Judgement », by Michelangelo (detail)

SISTINE CHAPEL. - « The Last Judgement », by Michelangelo (detail).

2) Creation of the Sun and Moon. 3) Creation of Trees and Plants. 4) Creation of Adam. 5) Creation of Eve. 6) The Fall and the Expulsion from Paradise (the serpent having a body of a female). 7) The Sacrifice of Noah and his family. 8) Deluge (this was the first subject which Michelangelo painted, and the proportions of the figures are not so colossal as in the others). Between the pilasters are the majestic figures of Prophets and Sibyls, and in the lunettes above the windows, the Ancestors of Christ. In the angular lunettes of the ceiling, above the altar to the left, Esther and Haman, to the right, the Brazen Serpent; to the left of the door, Judith and Holofernes; to the right, David and Goliath.

THE WALL BEHIND THE ALTAR. — Here we see the great fresco of the Last Judgment, the second masterpiece of Michelangelo in the Sistine Chapel. It occupies the entire wall (20 by 10 meters), and was commissioned by Clement VII. The artist, who was past sixty when he started it from 1535-1541 (seven years). In order to execute the work it was first necessary to wall-up two windows, and to destroy some frescoes of Perugino, and of Michelangelo himself. The stunning apocalyptic vision is admirable. To the right, the elect rise to the presence of God, the Father, and to the left, the damned descend to the eternal fires. In the center, Christ, the Judge rejects the condemned with a gesture. Grouped about him, the Madonna, and the Saints of the Old and the New Testments (Michelangelo's self-portrait is on the skin which Saint Bartholomew is holding in his hand). In the lower portion, between the sky and the earth, amidst the clouds, we see a troop of musical angels. To the right, the damned are reeling towards Hell, where the legendary Charon is waiting to ferry them across the river Styx. In a corner, the figure of Mides, with asses ears, is the likeness of the Master of Ceremonies of Paul III, who first suggested the indelicacy of the naked figures to the Pope (the painting narrowly escaped destruction). Later, by order of Pius IV, Daniele da Volterra covered the most prominent figures with drapery. To the left, the Resurrection of the flesh.

Leaving by the door to the right of the altar, we ascend to the next floor, and the Chapel of Saint Pius V. Two steps lead us next to the Stanze di Raffaello. (The Raphael Rooms).

SISTINE CHAPEL. - «God creates the Sun and Moon», by Michelangelo.

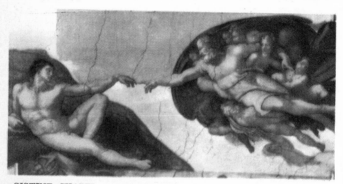

SISTINE CHAPEL. - « The Creation of Man », by Michelangelo.

SISTINE CHAPEL. - « Tre Original Sin and the Expulsion

ROOMS OF RAPHAEL. - « The fire of Borgo », by Raphael.

ROOMS OF RAPHAEL

Under the pontificate of Nicholas V, these rooms were
decorated by celebrated artists of the XV cent. Most of
these works, were destroyed, because Pope Julius II
(who had summoned Raphael from Florence to Rome, in
1508) was so delighted with his work that he wanted
the whole to be painted by him. The great master worked
here for the remainder of his life (d. 1520). It is one of
the masterpieces of world painting.

The first (but chronologically the last) is the *Stanza dell'Incendio*.
The major work here is the fresco on the wall opposite the
window, with the Incendio del Borgo (Fire in the Borgo). It is
inspired by the old legend that when the flames were raging
over the old district of Rome (« the Borgo »), they were miracu-

ROOMS OF RAPHAEL. - « The School of Athens », by Raphael.

ROOMS OF RAPHAEL. - « The Expulsion of Heliodorus after he had entered the Temple to steal », by Raphael.

lously stopped by Leo IV, who made the sign of the cross. Giulio Romano and F. Penni worked on this fresco too, as well as other pupils of the master. The remaining frescoes are by these pupils: the Incoronation of Charlesmagne; the Victory of Pius IV over the Saracens at Ostia; the Oath of Leo III. On the ceiling a fragment of the Trinity by Perugino (part of the decoration preceding Raphael's). - The next room is the *Stanza della Segnatura* (Room of the Signing of Papal Letters). This is the first room painted by Raphael (1508-11). On the wall near the entrance is the Dispute on the Sacrament (or the Triumph of Faith). On the opposite wall, the School of Athens, crowded with the greatest philosophers of ancient times, in a luminous and stately temple, inspired by Bramante's project of Saint Peter. In the center stand Plato and Aristotle. Plato is pointing towards heaven; Aristostle towards the earth. The solitary half-naked figure on the steps is Diogenes. Over the windows, Mt. Parnassus with Apollo, and the muses, and an assemblage of Greek, Roman and Italian poets. On the other wall the Delivery of the Pandects (civil law) and Decretals (canon law), fine works of Raphael. In the next *Stanza of Heliodorus*, painted by Raphael in 1512-14, we see some of the best works of the genius, featuring rich colouring, movement, contrasts of light and dark, and the grace which is the characteristic of this artist. On the wall of the entrance, Attila fleeing before Leo I. On the wall opposite the window, the Mass of Bolsena, with the miracle of the Host (a priest doubts the transubstantiation and is convinced by the blood which flows from the wafer he is consecrating). The kneeling personage praying on the other side of the altar is Julius II. On the left wall, the Expulsion of Heliodorus from the temple (among the spectators is Julius II, borne by his attendants on a chair of state). On the wall near the window, the Deliverance of Saint Peter from the Prison, with a remarkable effect of four lights. - Next we enter the *Sala of Constantine*, painted by Giulio Romano, F. Penni and Raffaellino del Colle (after Raphael's death). On the long wall opposite the window, the great fresco of the Battle of Constantine, or the Victory of Constantine over Maxentius at the Milvian Bridge. On the next wall, the Apparition of the Cross to Constantine, and on the wall near the window, Constantine Swearing Fidelity to the Pope.

CHAPEL OF NICHOLAS V

This chapel was decorated with frescoes between 1448-1451, by the Domenican Fra Giovanni da Fiesole, or the Beato Angelico. They represent scenes from the life of Saint Stephan, in the upper portion, and Saint Lawrence, in the lower portion. These works are suffused with a mystic quality and exquisite colour.

THE LOGGIA OF RAPHAEL

It faces the Court of Saint Damasus (1512-18 c.) and is divided into 13 arcades, with 48 scenes from the Old and New Testaments (the so-called Bible of Raphael). These were executed by the pupils of Raphael, Giulio Romano, Perin del Vaga, and F. Penni, from designs of the master. Most outstanding are: The Creation of the World; The Creation of Eve; The Deluge; Jacob's Dream; Moses Receiving the Tables of the Law; King David; The Birth of Jesus, and the Adoration of the Magi. The stucco decorations, and the grottesques of the mouldings, and the walls are by Giovanni da Udine.

The Gallery of Maps. — It is 120 meters long and is decorated with representations of the various regions of Italy, by Ignazio Dant, of Perugia (1580-83), the noted mathematician, cosmographer, and architect.

The Tapestry Gallery. — This Gallery contains 10 tapestries with scenes from the life of Jesus, from the so-called « New School » of the disciples of Raphael, and cloth fabricated in Brussels by Pieter van Aaelst (XVI cent.). The tapestry reproducing that Last Supper, by Leonardo, is from Fontainebleau (XVI cent.).

SEVENTH ITINERARY

Via del Corso - Doria-Pamphili Gallery - Sant'Ignazio - Piazza and Column of Marcus Aurelius - The Montecitorio Palace - The Fountain of Trevi - Quirinal Palace - Santa Maria della Vittoria - Porta Pia.

VIA DEL CORSO

It is the principal street of Rome, running in a straight line from Piazza Venezia, to the Piazza del Popolo; and then (the name changes to Via Flaminia) as far as the Milvio Bridge. It constitutes the axis of the city. Flanked by rich and stately palaces, this street in the Middle Ages, and at the height of the Baroque Period, was the scene of the famous Horse-races of the Carnival, in which Berber horses ran. The name of the street recalls these races.

Palazzo Doria. — At N. 34 of the Via del Corso, it was built in the XV cent. The beautiful facade, an excellent example of the rococò style, is the work of Valvassori, who constructed it circa 1730. The magnificent court, in the style of Bramante, is from the XVI cent. On the first floor of the palace is the *Doria-Pamphili Gallery;* (we enter the Gallery from the entrance at N. 1 Piazza del Collegio Romano). In this collection, are several masterpieces of Italian, and other schools of the XV to the XVII cent. The work includes the Portrait of Innocent X, by Velasquez; the Portrait of Two Gentlemen, by Raphael; Rest during the Flight into Egypt and a Madonna, by Caravaggio; Daughter of Herodias, by Titian, and other works by Correggio, Tintoretto, Mattia Preti, Parmigianino, N. Poussin, P. P. Rubens, etc.

Church of San Marcello. — This church was reconstructed in 1519 by Jacopo Sansovino; the baroque facade was designed by Fontana (1683). According to tradition, this church was constructed on the place where Emperor Maxentius forced Saint Marcello, while Pope, to groom horses in his stables (during which

DORIA GALLERY. - To the left: «Portrait of Joanna of Aragon», by Leonardo da Vinci; to the right: «Portrait of Andrea Doria», by Sebastiano del Piombo.

servitude he died). This supreme insult to the dignity of the Pope took place a short while before that atheist emperor was defeated by Constantine at the Battle of Milvio Bridge.

CHURCH OF SANT'IGNAZIO

This church was built between 1626-85, from designs of the Jesuit P. Orazio Grassi, inspired by Domenichino, to honour the sanctification of Ignatius of Loyola. The lofty facade is by Algardi.

The interior, with three naves, a transept, and an unfinished cupola, is rich with marble ornaments, and frescoes. The painting on the roof is a celebrated masterpiece of perspective, by Andrea Pozzo, portraying the Triumph of Saint Ignatius. A disc placed near the middle of the central nave, indicates the point from which this work may be enjoyed at its best. On the altar of the right transept, the Glory of San Luigi Gonzaga, a marble high - relief by P. Legros (XVII cent.). Beneath the altar, are the

143

remains of the Saint, in an urn of lapis-lazzuli. The monument to Gregory XV is in the next chapel, and by the same sculptor, P. Legros, the monument to Cardinal Ludovisi. On the altar of the left transept, a relief of the Annunciation, by F. Valle. The remains of San Giovanni Berghmans are in an urn beneath the altar.

Piazza Colonna. — In the form of a square, it constitutes one of the vital hubs of the city. On the side of the Corso, it is bound by the popular Colonna Gallery; on the right is a side the beautiful Palazzo Chigi. Further along, on the side, is the Neo-classic Wedekind Palace, also known as the Palace of the Portico of Veio, for the 16 Ionic columns of the Augustan Age, from Veio. In the center of the square, behind the elegant fountain of Giacomo della Porta (XVI cent.) rises the column of Marcus Aurelius, for which the square is named.

COLUMN OF MARCUS AURELIUS

Also known as the « Antoninus », the shaft is 29.60 meters high, and including the base, 42 meters high. It was erected between the years 176 and 193 A. D., and decorated with admirable bas-reliefs, to celebrate the victories of Marcus Aurelius over the Germans, and the Sarmatians. The spiral reliefs depict episodes of these wars of the Emperor. At the summit is the statue of Saint Paul, placed there by Sixtus V, in 1589, was the base restored by Domenico Fontana.

The Montecitorio Palace. — Continuing along one of the streets which flank the Wedekind Palace (with the 16 ionic columns from Veio, in the portico), we soon come to the Piazza Montecitorio. In the center of the Piazza stands the red granite Egyptian Obelisk of the period of Psammeticus I of the 26th dynasty, VI cent. B. C. It was originally brought to Rome by Augustus, from Heliopolis, and later placed here, in the square, by Pius VI, in 1789. On the north side of the square is the Montecitorio Palace, seat of the Chamber of Deputies (or House of Commons), begun in 1650, by Bernini, and finished in 1690, by Carlo Fontana. The modern facing, on the further side of the palace, is by E. Basile (1918).

PIAZZA COLONNA. - Colum of Marcus Aurelius.

Palazzo Chigi.

Largo Chigi. — At the north-east corner of Piazza Colonna is the Largo Chigi, facing which is the Chigi Palace, constructed for the famous Siennese bankers, in 1562, by Giacomo della Porta, and finished by Carlo Maderno. Further on, to the right, the *Church of Santa Maria in Via*, begun in 1594, by M. Longhi, the Elder, and finished by Carlo Rainaldi. - Continuing along this same via, turning to the left, we see the Fountain of Trevi.

THE FOUNTAIN OF TREVI

This is the largest and the most impressive of the famous fountains of Rome. (Behind the fountain is the facade of the Place of Dukes of Poli). This architectonic fantasy was commissioned by Clement XII, and executed by Nicola Salvi, (1762), who may have been inspired by a design of Bernini. In a large central niche, we see Neptune on his chariot drawn by marine horses, preceded by two tritons (the work of P. Bracci). In the niche to the left, the statue representing Abundance, to the right, Health (both are by F. Valle). The playful exuberance of these waters splashing over the rocks, to the center, and to the sides, create an unforgettable impression.

(The origin of the legend according to which all those who throw a coin into the fountain must return to Rome, is lost in the darkness of the Ages). The popular custom is for the visitor, with his back turned, to throw a coin into the fountain, and to make a vow to return.

PIAZZA DEL QUIRINALE

It is erected on the highest of the seven classic hills of Rome. At the center, we see the celebrated statue of the Dioscuri, Castor and Pollus, a Roman replica from the original Greek work of the IV-V cent. B. C. (found in the near-by Baths of Constantine). Between the statues is a slender obelisk, which once stood in the Mausoleum of Augustus. The piazza is bounded by the Quirinale Palace, on the further side; and by the baroque facade of the *Palazzo della Consulta*, built by Ferdinando Fuga, in 1734 for Clement XII. From the corner of Via XXIV Maggio, to the right, we can see the monumental entrance of Villa Colonna, and to the left, the 17th Cent. Pallavicini-Rospigliosi Palace that is on the site of the Baths of Constantine. In the court, to the left, (with special permission) one may visit the Casino. On the ceiling the famous fresco, The Aurora, by Guido Reni.

Quirinal Palace. — It was begun in 1574, by Gregory XIII, who built it as a summer residence for himself and for his successors. Among the architects who worked on this palace are (in chronological order), Flaminio Ponzio, O. Mascherino, Domenico Fontana, Carlo Maderno, and finally, it was completed by Ferdinando

Palazzo del Quirinale.

Fuga, in the XVIII cent. The façade of the palace is in the Renaissance style; with tympanum windows and architrave. On the left is a fortified glacis. Over the magnificent portal of Bernini, is a loggia resting on two harmonious columns, decorated with the statues of SS. Peter and Paul. First used as a summer residence of the Popes, it was, from 1870-1946, the residence of the King of Italy. Today it is the official palace of the President of the Republic. Within, the wide staircase is dominated by the great fresco of Melozzo da Forlì; Christ in Glory among Angels. Of special interest is the splendid Cuirassier Hall with richly decorated ceiling; the Pauline Chapel (which reproduces the celebrated Sistine Chapel of the Vatican) adorned with magnificent stucco work; the Annunciata Chapel, with an Annunciation by Guido Reni. In the other sumptuous halls, many works of art, and tapestries.

Proceding along the Via del Quirinale, which runs by the Quirinale Palace, we soon come to the Church of *Sant'Andrea al Quirinale*, built in 1678 by Bernini. The interior, of oval form, is richly scenic with marble and gilding, and celebrated paintings of Baciccia, Borgognone, and Maratta. - Further ahead, on the same side, is the Church of *San Carlino*, the first work of Borromini (1640), this church occupies precisely the same area as

Fontana di Trevi. (The Fountain of Trevi).

Trinità dei Monti.

one of the four piers which support the dome of St. Peters. Nearby is a small convent, with portico, and loggia. We are now at the characteristic crossroads of four streets known as the *Four Fountains* (with a fountain in each of the four corners). Here we have a perfect view of the street, constructed by Sixtus V, that connects the Pincio with Santa Maria Maggiore. In the distance, one may see simultaneously, the obelisk of the Esquiline, the Quirinale, and Trinità dei Monti. In Via XX Settembre (that is the continuation of Via del Quirinale) we see, in the distance, the Michelangioloesque Porta Pia. - Continuing along Via XX Settembre, we come to the spacious, picturesque Piazza San Bernardo. In the background, the *Fontanone dell'Acqua Felice*, by Domenico Fontana (1587); to the right, the *Church of San Bernardo*, constructed from one of the round halls which stood at the angles of the outer circuit of the Baths of Diocletian; to the left, the Church of *Santa Susanna*, of the III cent. (reconstructed in the XVI cent.) with a majestic facade by Carlo Maderno (1603). Nearby, the Church of Santa Maria della Vittoria.

Church of Santa Maria della Vittoria.

— Built by Carlo Maderno, in 1605, it has a beautiful facade, from the designs of G. B. Soria. The baroque interior is rich in precious marbles and decorations. In the second chapel to the right, an admirable painting by Domenichino; in the fourth chapel to the left, in the transept, the famous marble group of the Ecstasy of Saint Theresa, by Bernini.

Porta Pia.

— It is at the end of the Via XX Settembre. It was ordered by Pius IV in 1561, and built from the designs of Michelangelo (it was the last architectural work of the master). The external facade was added in 1868 by Vespignani.

Church of Sant'Agnese.

— After following the tree-lined Via Nomentana, for about two kilometers, we come to the Church of Sant'Agnese, more commonly known as S. Agnese Fuori le·Mura (outside the walls) to distinguish it from the other Sant'Agnese, in Piazza Navona. The basilica was built in 324, over the catacomb in which the young saint, martyred in 304, was buried. Remolded in the VII cent. it was subsequently restored many times, the last restoration being under Pius IX. We enter to the right of a small court, descending a long staircase whose walls are covered with marbles and inscriptions found in the catecombs. The interior, with three naves, is characteristic of the early Christian churches. The wooden ceiling is of the 17th cent.; the statue of Saint on the main altar is an antique

S. MARIA DELLA VITTORIA. - « St. **Theresa** », by Bernini.

torso of Roman alabaster, with modern head, hands and feet, by N. Cordier. Beneath the altar are the remains of Saint Agnes. On the vault of the tribune is an especially interesting mosaic portraying Saint Agnes, with the instruments of martyrdom, between Popes Symmachus and Honorius (635-38). In the left nave, is the entrance to the *Catacombs of S. Agnese*, the best preserved in the neighborhood of Rome, from the II-IV cent. Here we find epigraphic monuments of exceptional interest, and among the inscriptions is the epigraph of Pope Damaso, in honour of his martyrdom.

Church of Santa Costanza. — Ascending to the small court, we now walk down a small path to the Mausoleum of Costanza, the daughter of Constantine. It was built at the beginning of the IV cent. On the ceiling of the naves we see precious mosaics of the IV cent. These are the earliest known Christian series. In these mosaics, Christian symbols are combined with vintage scenes, and Bacchic motives of the pagan style. This round church-tomb is surmounted with a cupola which is supported by 24 coupled granite columns.

Piazza di Spagna.

EIGHTH ITINERARY

Piazza di Spagna - Trinità dei Monti - Palazzo Barberini - National Gallery - Via Veneto - Galleria Borghese - Museum of Villa Giulia - Santa Maria del Popolo - Piazza del Popolo - Mausoleum of Augustus.

PIAZZA DI SPAGNA

It is one of the most characteristic piazzas of Rome, named after the old Spanish Embassy to the Holy See that used to stand here. The monumental, celebrated, flight of 137 steps, *Scalinata della Trinità dei Monti*, which is opposite, was the work of Francesco de Sanctis and A. Specchi (1721-25). In the center of the piazza is a fountain popularly called « Barcaccia ». It was designed by Pietro Bernini, in commemoration of the great flood of 1598. On the right is the column of the Immaculate Conception (1865) erected by Pius IX. On the further

153

PIAZZA DI SPAGNA. - The Spanish Steps Trinità dei Monti.

side of the Piazza is the Palace of the « Propaganda Fide », the work of Bernini, 1627, and the center of the Catholic missions throughout the world. Borromini designed the dynamic facade of Via di Propaganda Fide.

PIAZZA DI SPAGNA. - Trinità dei Monti.

PIAZZA BARBERINI. - **Triton Fountain**, by Bernini.

TRINITA' DEI MONTI

At the top of the stairs of Trinità dei Monti, on the same level as the church, is a piazza from which we may enjoy a magnificent panorama of the city, and of the Piazza di Spagna, and Via Condotti, below. In the center of the Piazza is an Obelisk, which formerly stood in the gardens of Sallust. The Church of Trinità dei Monti was constructed by the French government between 1495-1585, destined for the use of the French residents of Rome. It has a picturesque facade flanked by two unusual bell-towers, attributed without foundation to Giacomo della Porta. Within the church, of special interest are the two paintings of Daniele da Volterra

VILLA BORGHESE. - The Lake.

the Descent from the Cross (his greatest masterpiece) in the second chapel to the left, and the Assumption, in the third chapel to the right (XVI cent.).

Via Sistina. — This aristocratic, quiet street of the 16th century, was the place of residence of many artists and intellectuals (especially in the XIX cent.). It connects Trinità dei Monti with Piazza Barberini.

Piazza Barberini. — In the midst of the piazza is the *Fontana del Tritone*, by Gian Lorenzo Bernini (1640), composed of four dolphins supporting an open shell, upon which sits a triton, who is blowing into the basin. In the background, to the right of the Piazza, we see a wing of the Palazzo Barberini.

PALAZZO BARBERINI

We enter from N. 13 via Quattro Fontane (one of the arteries of the city, instituted by Sixtus V). This baroque palace (a typical example of a sumptuous residence of a

NATIONAL GALLERY. - « Marriage of St. Catherine », by Sodoma.

Papal family) was begun by Carlo Maderno in 1625, with the help of Borromini, and finished in 1633 by Bernini. Bernini conceived the bold design of the tranverse portico between the two wings. The palace is the site of the National Gallery.

GALLERIA NAZIONALE

This important collection of paintings, (the National Gallery) occupies the first floor of the palace, and is composed of the bequests and donations of various persons, starting with the Cardinal Nero Corsini, and including the picture gallery of Prince Don Tommaso Corsini, the picture-gallery Torlonia, the Hertz Collection, etc.

From the portico on the ground floor, we ascend the superb winding staircase (also known as the Stairs of the Lion) by Bernini, and so reach the first floor, and the Picture Gallery. - Room I: works of the XIII-XIV cent. Crucifix, by Berlinghiero Berlinghieri; Madonna and Child, by Simone Martini; Stories of Christ, by G. Baronzio; Madonna, by M. Giambono; Incoronation, of the school of Orcagna. - Room II: works of Florentine artists of the XV cent. The Last Judgement, triptych of Beato Angelico; Madonna with Child, the first work of Filippo Lippi (1437), who is also the artist of the Annunciation; Portrait of a Lady, by Piero di Cosimo. - Room III: works of the XV cent. Madonna Villa Marina, by Piero della Francesca; Saint Nicholas of Tolentino, by Perugino; Madonna and Saints, by Lorenzo da Viterbo; Saint Sebastian and a Madonna, by Antoniazzo Romano. - Room IV: works of the XV-XVI cent. Saint George and the Dragon, by Francesco Francia; Christ in the Garden, by Bianchi Ferrari; Player of a Lute, by Andrea Solario; Portrait, by Bartolomeo Veneto; Sacred Conversation, by Lorenzo Lotto. - Room VII: Ceres by Baldassare Peruzzi; the Marriage of Saint Catherine, the Rape of the Sabines, and the Three Fates, by Sodoma. Room VIII: Madonna and Child, by Andrea del Sarto; the Holy Family, by Fra Bartolomeo; Portrait, by Pontormo; Portrait of Stefano Colonna, by Bronzino. - Room IX: La Fornarina, by Raphael; Pietà, by the Master of the Madonna of Manchester. Room X: the Portrait of Phillip II, by Titian; Christ and the Adultress, by Tintoretto; Nativity and the Baptism of Christ, by

BORGHESE GALLERY. - « Sacred and Profane Love », by Tiziano.

Theodokopuli, known as « El Greco. ». - Room XI: Venus and Adonis, replica of the work of Titian that is in the Prado of Madrid; the same subject by Luca Cambiaso; Adoration of the Sheperds, by Jacopo Bassano. - Room XII: various works of the school of Emilia, by Niccolò dell'Abate, Gerolamo da Carpi, and Passerotti. - Room XIII: Portrait of Bernardo Clesio, by J. van Clève; Portrait of Erasmus of Rotterdam, by Quentin Matsys. Room XIV: Portrait of Henry VIII; by H. Holbein, the Younger. Room XV: Saint John the Evangelist, by Dosso Dossi; Narcissus at the Fountain, by Caravaggio. - Room XVI: Holy Family, by Borgianni. - Room XVII: Portrait, by Baciccia; Portrait of a Gentleman, by Maratta. - Our visit ends with the great hall, the ceiling of which is by Pietro da Cortona, the Triumph of Providence (1633-38).

VIA VENETO

It is the most famous, and the most fashionable street of Rome, the center of many artistic activities, and the meeting place of the cosmopolitan set. Flanked by hotels, stores, luxurious cafès, this street is also the site of the graceful *Fontana delle Api* (Fountain of the Bees) by Bernini, (which is found at the beginning of the street, to the right), and; further ahead, on the same side, the Church of *Santa Maria della Concezione*, or « dei Cappuccini » constructed in 1624. Within this church are some admirable works of Domenichino, Gherardo delle Notti, and of Guido Reni, one of whose masterpieces is the Archangel Michael Killing the Demon. In the four chapels, which we may enter from the Sacristy, the walls are decorated with a macabre arrangement of bones and skulls, of 4.000 friars, who died in the adjoining convent. Still to the right of Via Veneto, at the second intersection, the *Palazzo Margherita*, built by G. Koch, in 1890; once the residence of Queen Margherita, and today the site of the American Embassy.

VILLA BORGHESE

It is the most picturesque public park of Rome. We enter from the *Porta Pinciana,* which is flanked by two cylindrical towers constructed under Balisarius (c. 546) at the period of the Gothic invasions. The complex of buildings and grounds which is Villa Borghese, was erected during the seventeenth century, by Cardinal Scipio Borghese. It occupies a vast area, for not only does it comprise a park with lush vegetation, but, in addition, various, museums, and a zoo. To the right of the large riding-ring, the Viale dell'Acqua Felix leads to the *Piazza di Siena,* which is surrounded by high pines, Here the horseraces are held. The Viale dell'Uccelliera leads to a square which is partly bounded by an ornate balustrade, and partly bounded by the Borghese Casino, which was built by Giovanni Vasanzio (1613-16). It is the site of the Galleria Borghese.

GALLERIA BORGHESE

Crossing the portico, and the entrance hall, impressive for the richness of its decoration, and for the pavement inlaid with mosaics of the IV cent., we reach the Museum. On the ground-floor is the Sculpture collection; on the first floor, the world-famous *Gallery* of paintings.

Room I: Pauline Borghese, the sister of Napoleon, a celebrated work by Antonio Canova (1805). - Room II: David and the slingshot, an early work of Gian Lorenzo Bernini (1619), (the David is a self-portrait). - Room III: Apollo and Daphne, the masterpiece of Bernini (1622). - Having traversed the chapel, frescoed with sacred as well as secular subjects, we reach Room IV or Emperors' Room, with busts of porphyry and alabaster, along the walls. These heads are of the XVII cent. In this room, another youthful work by Bernini, the Rape of Proserpine. - Room V: or the « Hermaphrodite Room ». - Room VI: Aeneas

163

BORGHESE GALLERY. - « Paolina Borghese », by Canova.

BORGHESE GALLERY. - To the left: « Young Lady with a Unicorn »,
by Raphael; to the right: « The Crucifixion », by Pintoricchio.

BORGHESE GALLERY. - To the left: « **St. Stephen** », by Francia to the right: « **Madonna and Child** », by Bellini.

BORGHESE GALLERY. - To the left: « **Portrait of a Young Man** », by Antonello da Messina; to the right: « **St. John the Baptist's Prayer** », by Veronese.

and Anchises, a marble group of Pietro Bernini, in collaboration with his son; Truth discovered by Time, an unfinished composition by Bernini, who began it in 1645. - Room VII: or the « Egyptian Room », with statues of Isis and Ceres and an Egyptian sphinx in basalt. - Room VIII: the Dancing Faun, Roman copy of a bronze original, by Lysippus.

From the Emperors' Room, we ascend a winding staircase to the first floor and the collection of fine paintings of the Galleria Borghese. At the entrance, the Three Ages of Man, by Sassoferrato; Venus and Love, by Luca Cambiaso; Psyche, by Iacopo Zucchi. - Room IX: Portrait of a Young Woman with Unicorn, Portrait of a Man, and the Deposition, three works by Raphael; the Crucifixion with SS. Jerome and Christopher, by Pintoricchio; Madonna and Child, Saint John and Angels, by Botticelli; Madonna by Perugino. - Room X: Pietà by Sodoma; Portrait of a Man, by A. Dürer; Venus and Love, by Lucas Cranach; Madonna and Child by Andrea del Sarto. In addition, the oustanding canvases with the Labours of Hercules, by Cristoforo Unterberger (7186). Room XI: Holy Conversation, by Lorenzo Lotto; the Return of the Prodigal Son, by Antonio Palma; Tobias and the Angel, by G. Savoldo. - Room XII: Portrait of Marcello Sacchetti, by Pietro da Cortona; Sibyl, by Domenichino; Flight into Egypt, bp the Cavalier d'Arpino. - Room XIII: Madonna and Child, by Giulio Romano, and works of Pellegrino Tibaldi, Bacchiacca, and artists of the XVI cent. - Room XIV: Madonna dei Palafrenieri, David with the head of Goliath, Young Bacchus, Young Boy with Basket of Friut, Saint Jerome, all works of Caravaggio; the Hunt of Diana, by Domenichino; Christ being brought to the Tom, by Carracci. In addition five sculptures by Gian Lorenzo Bernini, including the busts of Cardinal Scipione Bolognese, and the model for the equestrian statue to Louis XIV. - Room XV: Lamentation for the death of Christ, by Rubens; two Self-Portraits, and the Portrait of a Young Boy, three canvases by Gian Lorenzo Bernini; Orpheus, by Breughel. - Room VI: Adoration of he Shepherds, by Iacopo Bassano; Sleeping Venus, by Girolamo Savoldo; the Fall of Lucifer, by Palma the Younger. - Room XVII: Saint Stephen, by F. Francia; the Deposition, by Ortolano. - Room XVIII: dedicated to non-Italian artists. Susanna and the Elders, by Rubens; Drinkers, by Teniers. - Room XIX: Danae, by Correggio; the Enchantress Circe, by Dosso Dossi. - Room XX: Sacred and Profane Love, by Titian, and also by Titian, Venus and Love; Saint John the Baptist Baptist Preaching, by Paolo Veronese; Portrait of a Man, by Antonello da Messina; Portrait of a Youth, by Palma, the Elder, Madonna, by Giovanni Bellini; Cortesan, by Carpaccio; Giorgione, Two Men.

Zoological Gardens. — This is the largest zoological park in Italy, and is located on the grounds of the Villa Borghese. Here we may see a collection of indigenous and exotic animals, that is being continuosly enriched by specimens which arrive from all parts of the globe.

Galleria d'Arte Moderna. — This is located in the large Palazzo delle Belle Arti, built by Cesare Bazzani in 1911, and amplified by him in 1933. It is considered the most important collection of Italian painting and sculpture of the XIX cent. and of the XX cent.

MUSEUM OF VILLA GIULIA

It is located in the Palazzo di Villa Giulia, built by Julius III in 1533. The dignified and severe aspect of this palace, enlivened only by the small loggia in the center of the facade, is the work of Ammannati: the interior, fantastic, with a magnificent nympheum beyond a great, arcade court, is the work of Vignola.

This archaeological museum is divided in five sections: the *Topographical Museum of Southern Etruria, execepting Veio*, which is on the ground floor, in the north wing; the *Antiquarium of Bronzes, Glass and Terracottas*, in the upper galleries of the north wing; the *Antiquarium of Ceramics and Gold-work*, and the *Topographical Museum of the Territory of Veio*, on the first floor the villa; *Topographic Museum of the Falerian Territory*, in the upper galleries of the south wing; the *Topographical Museum of Lazio and Umbria*, on the groundfloor of the southwing. The five sections comprise 34 rooms, in addition to some minor areas within, and outside the building.

Of special interest: Room I: the archaic statue (VI cent. B.C.) of a Centaur, and of a Man on a Marine Monster; the Ara Guglielmi, an exceptional funerary monument composed of a little chapel with four square columns, and composite capitals. - Room VI: three great clay statues from the Sanctuary of Apollo at Veio: Apollo, Hercules with a Deer; and Goddess with child, masterpieces of Etruscan sculpture of the VI cent. B.C. - Room VII: objects from the city and the ancient necropoli of Cerveteri, including a beautiful group of Amazons with horses (terracotta of the VI cent. B.C.); a dynamic Portrait of

BORGHESE GALLERY. - « Madonna with Saints », by Lotto.

BORGHESE GALLERY. - To the left: « Madonna and Child », by Perugino; to the right: « Madonna and Child », by Andrea del Sarto.

SAN PIETRO IN VINCOLI. - « Moses », by Michelangelo.

a Man, from the Temple of Manganello. - Room VIII: the so-called sarcophagus of the « married-couple », a masterpiece of Etruscan sculpture of the second-half of the VI cent. B.C.

Pincio. — This very famous garden, on the Pincian Hill, was laid-out in the XIX cent. by Valadier, in the neo-classic style. In antiquity this was the site of sumptuos patrician villas. From the wide terrace, that overlooks the Piazza del Popolo, we may enjoy one of the most beautiful and one of the most unforgettable views of the city. To the right, Monte Mario and the districts on the other side of the Tiber; straight ahead the cupola of Saint Peter's; in the distance, the Janiculum Hill, the Vittoriano, the Quirinal Palace.

Villa Medici. — This building was constructed, in an austere style, towards the middle .of the XVI cent., by A. Lippi, for the Cardinal Ricci. In the XVII cent. it was acquired by the Medici, and used as the residence of their cardinals. Napoleon, in 1803, made it the site of the French Academy, founded by Louis XIV, in 166. Here, the young French artists, who win the « Prix de Rome » spend three years in a course of specialization.

Porta del Popolo. — It rises on the same site as the ancient Porta Flaminia of the Aurelian Wall, and it was built in 1561, by Vignola, who framed the arch with ancient columns. The internal facade was decorated by Bernini in 1655, on the occasion of the arrival in Rome of Christina of Sweden.

SANTA MARIA DEL POPOLO

It is on the site of a small chapel erected by Paschal II, towards the end of the XI cent. The architects, Baccio Pontelli, and Andrea Bregno restored it in 1477, under Sixtus IV, in the Renaissance style, with a simple facade and two orders of columns. The Papal families not only embellished this church, but also erected their tombs here. The gabled bell-tower, on the right side, is a characteristic feature.

The interior has three naves with the roof supported by pilasters, and a cupola over the transept. Althought it has later Baroque embellishments, it still maintains its Renaissance character. The first chapel of the right nave, dedicated to the Della Rovere Family, is completely decorated in frescoes by Pintoricchio (1485-89) portraying scenes from the life of St. Jerome. Of the same artist is the altar-screen with the Adoration of the Child. Along the left wall, the Tomb of Cardinal Della Rovere, by Mino da Fiesole, and Andrea Bregno (XV cent.). - The second chapel of the Cybo family, was redecorated by Carlo Fontana in the XVII cent. On the altar, is a painting of the Assumption, by Maratta. - The third chapel is decorated with frescoes by Pintoricchio, and others, including Tiberio d'Assisi (1504-7). Above the altar, the Madonna and Child, and on the left wall, beneath the Assumption, the Tomb of Cardinal Foscari, a bronze work attributed to Vecchietta (XV cent.). Above the altar of the fourth chapel, a marble triptych of the school of Bregno, and frescoes of the school of Pintoricchio. - On the main altar, a painting of the Madonna, in the Byzantine style of the XIII cent.; at the sides of the presbytery, two beautiful sepulchral monuments by Sansovino; on the ceiling, the magnificent frescoes of Pintoricchio (1508-9). The apse is the work of Bramante; the stained-glass is by Guglielmo di Marsiglia (1509-10). On the side walls of the chapel to the left of the presbytery are two great masterpieces of Caravaggio: the Crucifixion of Saint Peter, and the Conversion of Saint Paul. - The Chigi chapel, the second of the left nave, adorned in the elegant, style of the Renaissance was constructed from the designs of Raphael, who also designed the mosaics of the cupola, and the statues of the prophets, Jonah, and Elias, which were executed by Lorenzetto. Daniel and Habakkuk are by Bernini, the bronze-relief on the altar-front is by Lorenzetto. The painting of the Nativity of the Virgin is by Sebastiano del Piombo. Along the side walls, the tombs of the Chigi family, in pyramidal form. In the adjacent convent of the order of St. Augustine, Martin Luther resided when he visited the city.

PIAZZA DEL POPOLO

This architectonic, impressive piazza was designed by G. Valadier, at the beginning of the XIX cent. He also designed the magnificent winding ascent, to the Pincio. The piazza is embellished at the sides with two hemicycles decorated ith statues and fountains. The site of

171

SAN PIETRO IN VINCOLI. - The Chains of St. Peter.

the church was formerly, according to legend, the burial-
ground of the Domitius family, and it was here, that
Atte deposited the ashes of Nero. Because the ghost of
the demonic emperor was said to be molesting the people
of the area, Pope Paschal II, in 1099, ordered the demoli-
tion of the mausoleum, and on the spot, he consecrated
a small chapel that was later transformed into the present
church by Sixtus IV. In the center of the piazza, an
Egyptian Obelisk, 24 meters high, (36.50 including
the pedestal) from the time of Rhameses II (XIII
cent. B.C.). This obelisk was removed from Helio-
polispolis to Rome, by order of Augustus, and erected
in the Circus Maximus. Sixtus V, in 1585, placed it in
its present site. At the south side of the piazza, at the
intersection of Via del Corso, are two symmetrical baro-

Santa Maria Maggiore.

SANTA MARIA MAGGIORE. - Interior.

que churches, with two picturesque cupolas: *Santa Maria dei Miracoli* (1678) and *Santa Maria in Montesanto* (1675); both begun by C. Rainaldi, and finished by Bernini and Carlo Fontana.

MAUSOLEUM OF AUGUSTUS

It is in the center of a wide piazza. Constructed by the Emperor Augustus, it was to be used a sepulchre for himself, and for the imperial family (27 B. C.). Originally, an impressive structure of a round shape, rich in marbles and statues, bounded by porticoes, crowned by a conical mound of earth, with cypresses, at the top, there was a statue of the Emperor. In the Middle Ages, it was converted into a fortress, and in later periods, used for other purposes. In 1936 it was restored. Within, we may see the crypt in which were placed the urns.

ARA PACIS AUGUSTAE

It is at the base of a pavilion, which is to the left of Via Ripetta. First built in 13 B.C., to honour the Emperor, and the long, prosperous period of peace, he had given Rome, it was accurately reassembled in 1938, using the original fragments, which had been kept in the National Museum. The outer part is almost completely covered with a frieze, and with bas-reliefs illustrating the deeds of the Emperor: the Fertile Earth; Scenes of Sacrifice, and imperial Procession of Augustus, and Members of his family.

NINTH ITINERARY

San Pietro in Vincoli - Santa Maria Maggiore - Baptistry of San Giovanni - San Giovanni in Laterano - The Museums of the Lateran - Santa Croce in Gerusalemme - San Lorenzo fuori le Mura.

SAN PIETRO IN VINCOLI

Also known as the *Basilica Eudoxiana*, it was built in 442, by Eudoxià, wife of Valentinian III, to preserve the chains with which St. Peter was bound at Palestine, and at Rome. The church was restored in 1475, under Sixtus IV, and modernized in the XVIII cent.

The stately interior consists of three naves divided by ancient columns. Near the end of the right aisle is the Mausoleum of Julius II, with the celebrated statue of Moses, by Michelangelo (c. 1513) constituting a perfect fusion of the style of the Renaissance, with the Baroque. The original plan, ordered by Julius II, was for a magnificent tomb, of vast proportions, adorned with 44 statues (one of which is the Moses), to be designed by Michelangelo. But the design, due to various vicissitudes, was never completed. Of the statues partly finished by Michelangelo, are the famous « Captives », in Florence, and in Paris. The two statues at the sides, Leah and Rachel, were begun by Michelangelo, but finished by pupils, who also finished the other work. Beneath the main altar, in a beautiful bronze tabernacle, with reliefs attributed to Caradosso (1477) are preserved the chains of St. Peter. - At the second altar of the left nave, a Byzantine mosaic portraying St. Sebastian, of the VII cent.

San Giovanni in Laterano.

SAN GIOVANNI IN LATERANO. - Interior.

SANTA MARIA MAGGIORE

It is called « Maggiore » because it is the largest church in Rome that is dedicated to the Madonna. It is also called the basilica « Liberiana », from a tradition that on the 5th of August, 352, the Madonna appeared in a vision to Pope Liberius and to John, a Roman patrician, and ordered them to build a church on the spot where snow would fall the following day. (Research indicates, however, that the church was founded by Sixtus III, soon after 431). The majestic apse, flanked by the cupolas of the two great chapels, was remodeled in the XIII cent.; the back of the church in the 1600's. The principal facade, a wide loggia, and three spacious arcades enclosed by two structures, is a spirited work by Ferdinando Fuga (1743); who was commissioned by Benedict XIV. To the right, is the peaked Romanesque bell-tower, (1377) that is the highest in Rome. In the portico, to the right, is the statue of Phillip IV, by G. Lucenti (1692); a disciple of Bernini. In the loggia are found admirable mosaics, that once formed part of the ancient facade, portraying the vision of Pope Liberius.

The interior, 86 meters long, follows the basilica plan of construction of the Early churches. The three spacious naves are separated by Ionic columns which support the architrave. The pavement of the central nave is Cosmatesque (XII cent.), and the rich coffered, roof attributed to Giuliano da Sangallo, is from the beginning of the XVI cent. The square panels of mosaic, above the columns, represent scenes from the lives of Abraham, Isaac and Jacob (V cent.). From the same period, are mosaics on the face of the triumphal arch, outside the tribune, portraying scenes from the infancy of Jesus. The main altar is covered by a baldacchino supported by four porphyry columns, the work of Fuga. At the from is the Confession, a rich reconstruction of 1864, by Vespignani, wherein are preserved the sacred relics of the Manger of Bethlehem. The kneeling statue of Pius IX is by I. Iacometti (1860). The apse of the tribune is covered by wonderful mosaics portraying the Triumph of the Virgin, by Iacopo Torritti (1295). - In the right nave is the rich

S. MARIA MAGGIORE. - Monument to Pius V.

S. MARIA MAGGIORE. - Monument to Paul V.

Sistine Chapel (or « of the Sacrament »), designed by Domenico Fontana (1586), a majestic work of art, of harmonious lines, and proportions. On the Papal Altar is the bronze tabernacle supported by four angels. On the right wall, the funerary monument so Sixtus V; on the left wall, the monument to Pius V, both works of Fontana. In the crypt of the altar is the Oratory of the altar is the Oratory of the Manger, with a group of archaic style statues, by Arnolfo di Cambio (XIII cent.). Towards he end of the right nave is the beautiful Gothic tomb of Card. Consalvo Rodriguez, by Giovanni Cosma (c. 1299). On the opposite side is the *Chapella Paolina* or Borghesana, built by Paul V, from the designs of Flaminio Ponzio (1611) and said to be one of the most beautiful chapels in the world. Above the altar, a Madonna, in the Byzantine style of the XIII cent. On the left wall, a monumental Tomb of Paul V; on the right, Tomb of Clement VIII. Both are covered with bas-reliefs. The frescoes of the walls are by Guido Reni, while those of the pendentives, beneath the cupola, are by the Cavalier d'Arpino. Beneath, are the sepulchral vaults of the Borghese family. - At the beginning of the right nave is the entrance to the Baptistery, where we find, on the altar, the bas-relief of the Assumption, by P. Bernini (1606-11).

Piazza dell'Esquilino. — Spacious and luminous, this square is dominated by the apse of Santa Maria Maggiore. In the center, stands an *Obelisk* which originally flanked the entrance to the Mausoleum of Augustus, and which was erected here, by Sixtus V, in 1587. At the junction of the square and Via Urbana, is the Church of *Santa Pudenziana*, with a beautiful bell-tower of the XIIcent., and an ancient Romanesque portal. It is one of the oldest churches of Rome, having been founded by Pope Siricio in the IV cent. Within the church, in the Tribune, is a precious mosaic. of the IV cent. portraying Christ surrounded by Apostles. The cupola was painted by Pomarancio.

Santa Prassede. — It was built in the V cent., and dedicated to the sister of Santa Pudenziana. Reconstructed by Paschal I, in 822, it was, subsequently, many times restored. The interior, rich in valuable mosaics of the IX cent. consists of three naves divided by 16 columns and six piers. In the right nave, is the Chapel of St. Zeno, the most notable feature of this church, erected by Paschal I, as a mausoleum for his mother, Theodora. It is Byzantine in style. Above the columns of the doorway are two rows of mosaics: the Madonna and Child, with SS. Pudenziana, and Prassede; and Christ with the Apostles and Saints.

The mosaics covering the walls and the ceiling are adorned with figures. In a niche, is the column, brought from Jerusalem, at which Christ was scourged, so says the tradition. On the triumphal arch of the presbytery are mosaics of the time of Pope Pascal I (817-824). They depict the New Jerusalem and Jesus among Saints; in the arch of the apse, the Saviour between SS. Paul, Prassede and Paschal; to the right: SS. Peter, Pudenziana and Zeno; below: the Jordan, and a lamb bearing a cross, with six sheep, emblemetical of Christ and the Apostles.

Piazza San Giovanni in Laterano. — In the center rises an Egyptian Obelisk, of red granite, which is the highest, and the most ancient of Rome (31 meters high; 47 including the base). Erected in the IV cent. B.C., at Thebes, in Egypt, where it stood in the temple of Amun, brought to Rome by Constantinus II, and placed in the Circus Maximus, in 357, it was removed to its present site by Sixtus V, in 1588. The stately Lateran Palace it to the right of the piazza, at the side of the church. The lateral facade of the church near the palace, with a double portico, was constructed by Domenico Fontana (1586). Above it rise two bell-towers of the XII cent. Further to the right, the Lateran Atheneaum, and the Baptistry.

BATTISTERO DI SAN GIOVANNI

The Baptistry of Saint John was originally constructed by Constantine, and restored in the V cent. by Sixtus III. The interior of this octagonal building is divided into two concentric naves, with eight columns of porphyry that sustain a handsome architrave. Above rises the cupola on an octagonal drum. In the center is a Baptismal Font of green basalt about which are clustered four chapels. The first chapel, to the right, is dedicated to Saint John the Baptist, and features an ancient bronze door, which swinging on its hinges, is said to emit a musical sound. The bronze doors are said to have been brought from the Baths of Caracalla. In the second chapel is a Crucifix of the XVI cent.; a Saint Phillip by Guido

S. GIOVANNI IN LATERANO. - Monument to Innocent III.

S. GIOVANNI IN LATERANO. - Monument to Leo XIII.

Reni and mosaics of the IV-V cent. These are among the most ancient Christian mosaics of Rome. In the third chapel, remarkable mosaics of the VII cent. In the fourth chapel, a bronze door of 1196, mosaics on the ceiling, and a bronze statue of Saint John, by L. Lantini.

SAN GIOVANNI IN LATERANO

This cathedral of Rome rises on the site of the ancient palace of Plautinus Lateranus (hence the name), one of the noblest families of Rome. Plautinus Lateranus conspired against Nero, and for this reason all the property of the family was confiscated, but, later, the palace was returned to the Laterans, forming part of the dowry of Fausta, the daughter of Maximus Erculeaum and the wife of Constantine. After Constantine became converted to Christianity, he donated the buildings to the church, to be used as an episcopal residence, and here, a great church, dedicated by Pope Melchiades (311-14), was built. Many times destroyed, and many times restored, it was abandoned after the Holy See was transferred to Avignon, and after a disastrous fire, in 1308, almost destroyed the great building. Reconstructed by Urban V, in the XIV cent., it was decorated by Borromini (1646-49) under Innocent X. The majestic front of the church is by Alessandro Galilei (1735), and is dominated by the Statue of the Saviour, on the balustrade, flanked by 14 statues of apostles and saints. In the vestibule, to the left, is the ancient marble statue of Constantine, from his Bath on the Quirinale, placed here by Clement XII. The central bronze door is from the Curia di Ostilia (ancient Senate - House).

The interior, in the form of a Latin cross, has 5 naves. It is 130 meters long. The central nave is 87 meters long, and flanked by great piers, in which are 12 niches, containing Statues of the Apostles (18th cent.). The marvelous wooden ceiling is from the 1500's, and is ornamented with symbols of the church, and of the Passion. The Cosmatesque pavement dates from the time of Martin V (1450). At the beginning of the right nave is the Orsini Chapel, and further ahead, to the left, on the first pier, a fresco, portraying Boniface VIII proclaiming the Jubilee of 1300, attributed to Giotto. Along the walls and within the chapels, there are many noteworthy tombs from the XIII to the XVIiI century. In the extreme left nave, the first chapel, dedicated to Sant'Andrea Corsini, a noble and harmonious work of Alessandro Galilei (1734). Within, to the left, the tomb of Clement XII, containing a porphyry urn, from the Pantheon. On the central altar, a great mosaic representing Saint Andrew, by Cristifori (from the original by Guido Reni). Worthy of admiration is the gate of gilt bronze. The most beautiful, and the most interesting part of the church is the vast transept, which is richly decorated with marbles, and frescoes portraying the « Leggenda Aurea » of Constantine. Within the high Papal altar is conserved a table of wood, on which St. Peter is said to have celebrated Mass. It is surmounted by a Gothic canopy, erected in 1367, by Urban V, and decorated externally by frescoes attributed to Barna da Siena ,and restored by Antoniazzo Romano (XV cent.). The great mosaic of the apse, is a reproduction of the original executed by Iacopo Torriti in the XIII cent. To the left of the tribune, the monument to Leo XIII, by Tadolini, and at the end of the transept, the beautiful Chapel of the Sacrament, by Paolo Olivieri (1599) is flanked by four columns of bronze, plated with gold, that were transferred from the Campidoglio, by Constantine. To the right of the tribune, the monument to Innocent III, by Giuseppe Lucchetti (1891), from the period of Leo XIII. Further to the right, the Chapel of the Crucifix, containing the Cosmatesque figure of Boniface IX; the work of an unknown artist.

From the last chapel of the extreme left nave, which is dedicated to Saint Illarius, and which has a fresco by Borgognone above the altar, we enter the beautiful Cloister, which is decorated with small, binate columns, and which is the masterpiece of Vassalletto (1222-30). For beauty, this architecture ranks with Saint Paul. The well, in the center, is from the period of Pascal I (IX cent.). Under the portico is a papal throne, and the remains of a monument to Cardinale Annibaldi, by Arnolfo di Cambio (1277).

THE MUSEUMS OF THE LATERAN

These are in the Lateran Palace, and comprise a collection that was put together from the first half of the 1800's, to the first 30 years of this century. In 1844, Gregory XVI inaugurated the Museo Profano of ancient Roman and Greek sculptures; ten years later, under Pius IX, the Christian Museum was opened to the public, and in 1926, under Pius XI, the Missionary Museum of Ethnology was instituted.

MUSEO PROFANO. — We cross the great court, and enter from the corridor to the left. The museum, which is composed of 16 rooms, comprises material from the Vatican collection, subsequently enriched by the fruits of later excavations. Of exceptional interests, in Room I: copies of Greek statue of the IV cent. B.C. - Room II: a series of capitals and architectural friezes, from Trajan's Forum. - Room III: Antinous in the guise of Vertunno (II cent. A.D.) - Rooms IV-V: mosaics from the pavements discovered in 1824, in the Baths of Caracalla (III cent. A.D.); cinerary urn with the head of Medusa, and a cock-fight (I cent. A.D.); two urns of the Faun, with young Dionysius (I cent. A.D.) - Room VI: statues and reliefs from the Roman theater at Cerveteri (I cent. A.D.). - Room VII: reliefs of Medea and the daughters of Pelias, probably from a Greek original of the V cent. B.C.; Sophocles, copy of the original Greek of the IV cent. B.C.; reliefs with Menander and Comedy, Hellenistic art of the I cent. B.C. - Room VIII: series of sepulchral monuments of the Ateri family (I cent. A.D.). - Room IX: reconstructed mosaic pavement of Heraclitus of the II cent. A.D., found in 1833 on the Aventine. - Room X: colossal statue of Neptune, god of the sea, from an original of the I cent. B.C. - Room XI: Roman sarcophagi from the II to the III cent. A.D. - Room XII: Round altar dedicated to the goddess Pietà, of the I cent. A.D.; sarcophagus with the myth of Niobe (II cent. A.D.) - Room XIII: sepulchral reliefs and fragments of statues. - Room XIV: Cinerary urns of the I - II cent. A.D., and an unfinished statue of Dace (II cent. A.D.) - Room XV: fragments of sarcophagi; funerary urns; bronze statuettes of Venus; niche in mosaic, representing Silvanus with his dog, from the II cent. A.D. - Room XVI: fragments of frescoes, urns, statues and sepulchral fragments .- Returning to the vestibule, from which we entered, under the portico, we find the *Pagan Epigraph Collection*.

THE CRISTIAN MUSEUM. — We enter from the portico to the left of the entrance of the palace. This museum comprises a collection of material from the catacombs of Rome, and from the ancient churches, in addition to the Museum of Christian Epigraphy, with inscriptions of the I to the VI cent.

THE MISSIONARY MUSEUM OF ENTHNOLOGY. — The entrance is opposite the Museo Profano. This museum contains documents relating to the work of missionaries, and interesting curios of the various peoples, among whom the missionaries work.

Scala Santa. — To the left of the piazza is the 16th cent. structure wherein are conserved the stairs, which according to tradition, are the identical ones which Jesus ascended when he was presented to Pilate for judgement. They were brought to Rome by the Empress Helen. They consist of 28 steps, protected by planks of wood; and they may ascended by the faithful, on their knees. The stairs lead to the chapel dedicated to Saint Lawrence, which is what remains of the ancient palace of the Popes, the *Sancta Sanctorum*. It contains a great number of sacred relics, and is ornamented with beautiful Cosmatesque mosaics (1276). The chapel, which may also be reached by a stairway at the side, is always closed, and may only be viewed through the grating of the small windows.

SANTA CROCE IN GERUSALEMME

It is one of the churches founded by Constantine, and built by Saint Helen, the mother of Constantine, circa 320, to preserve the relics of the Passion which she had brought from Jerusalem. The church underwent frequent alterations, the most notable taking place in 1144, under Lucius II, when it was converted into a Romanesque structure, and the present bell-tower was built. The present facade, and the portico, in the Baroque style, were constructed by the architects Gregorini and Passalacqua, in 1743, under Benedict XIV. The pavement is Cosmatesque. The frescoes, in the apse, representing the Discovery, the History, and the Triumph of the Cross, are by Antoniazzo Romano, of the school

S. CROCE IN GERUSALEMME. - To the left: **The Facade**;
to the right: **Relics of the Passion**.

of Pintoricchio (latter part of the XV cent.). Beneath the
painting, in the center, is the monument to Cardinal F.
Quiñones, by Iacopo Sansovino (1563). To the right,
and to the left, are frescoes representing the Serpent of
Bronze, and Moses striking water from the rock, by
G. Giaquinto (1744). Above the second altar to the right
is a painting by Maratti (1660). From the transept, we
enter a chapel which is richly adorned with marble
(1930), in which is preserved the cross-beam of the cross
of the Good Robber (San Disma). From this chapel, a
stairway leads to the Chapel of the Holy Relics. To
the left is the reliquary with a collection pertaining to
the Saints and martyrs, which formerly belonged to
Saint Gregory the Great; in the center is a Byzantine
mosaic (XI cent.) portraying the « Ecce Homo »; at the

further and are some precious reliquaries containing: three notable fragments of the Cross (the largest in the world), a piece of the tablet on which was inscribed the title of the Cross, a nail, two thorns from the crown, a phalange from the finger of Saint Thomas, and, in addition, fragments from the columns of the Flagellation, of the grotto of the Nativity, and of the Sepulchre. From the left side of the apse, we enter the Chapel of Saint Helen, the ceilling of which is decorated with an original mosaic of the V cent., restored in the XVI cent., from the designs of Melozzo da Forlì. On the walls are traces of the 16th cent. frescoes by Pomarancio and by Circignani, which have been almost completely destroyed by saltpetre. In this chapel, Saint Helen, deposited the relics of the Passion, and they remained here until 1570. The statues of the saint dates from the Roman period, and was discovered at Ostia, minus the head and the arms. The chapel opposite, known as the « Pietà », is named after the bas-relief (of an unknown • sculptor), dating from the latter part of the XVI cent., and portraying the Deposition. To the sides of the altar are two small statues of SS. Peter and Paul, of the French school, of the XIV cent.

SAN LORENZO FUORI LE MURA

It is to the rear of the square which is in front of the Cemetery of *Campo Verano*. The church which is one of the seven principal churches of Rome, is actually a combination of two churches, of two different periods: the ancient one built by Constantine in 330, and reconstructed by Pelagius II, in 578; the other facing in the opposite direction, probably built by Adrian I in the VIII cent. and joined to the old church which became the presbytery of the new complex. It was restored in the XV and the XVII cent., and has been restored once again. The facade, framed by cypresses, with its Romanesque bell-tower of the XII cent., is preceded by a beautiful portico of Vassalletto (1220), with six columns of ancient marble, supporting an architrave of marble with frieze.

The interior consists of three naves separated by ancient columns. On the entrance wall, are the only remains of the celebrated frescoes of Fracassini (the rest have been destroyed). They have been transferred on canvas. Half-way down the nave are two ambones. Particularly beautiful is the one the right, rich in marbles and mosaics, and with small columns for the paschal wax, the work of Cosmati (XII-XIII cent.). A great arch, decorated with imitation mosaics on a gold background, frames the presbytery. We climb the steps to the présbytery of the old church, built by Pelagius II, which has two rows of superimposed columns. In the lower row, slender light fluted columns of pavonazzetto from the women's gallery are crowned with Corinthian capitals. On the face of the original Chancel Arch, which was in the Church of Pelagius II, is the great mosaic, of the Byzantine school, portraying Christ enthroned, with the Cross in his left hand, surrounded by Saints. It dates from the VI cent. Towards the back of the presbytery is the rich Papal Throne decorated with patterns of porphyry, and precious polychrome marbles.

Behind it is a splendid transenna. Crossing the Sacristy, which we enter from the right nave, we come to the exquisite cloister, a gem of Romanesque art (1241).

TENTH ITINERARY

**Via San Gregorio - SS. Giovanni e Paolo - Baths
of Caracalla - Porta San Sebastiano - San Clemente.**

Via San Gregorio. — It begins at the Arch of Constantine
and runs along the slopes of the Palatine. To the right are the
ruins of the aqueduct of Claudius; to the left, the aqueduct
of the Caelian. In ancient times, triumphal processions would
proceed down this street, and for that reason, it was called
the *Via Triumphalis*.

San Gregorio Magno. — This church, founded by Pope Gregory, at the same period as the monastery (590-604), rises on a
site which is picturesque and peaceful. The original structure,
which had already been restored after the XI cent. was embellished by G.B. Soria (1633). He added the Baroque facade, and
the impressive stairway. Crossing the rectangular atrium, we
enter the 18th cent. interior of the church, which has three naves,
separated by ancient columns. At the end of the right aisle is
the Altar of Saint Gregory with bas-relief on the altarfront
representing three periods from the life of the saint. To the
right is the little room where the Papal Saint lived in poverty.
Here is conserved his marble episcopal chair. - To the left of
the church, a gate leads into a court, in which there are three
small chapels: in the chapel to the right is a fresco of a Concert
of Angels, by Guido Reni; in the central chapel, frescoes by
Domenichino, and Reni; in the chapel to the left, the great
marble table, on which St. Gregory fed 12 paupers every morning.

SS. Giovanni e Paolo. — This church rises on a scenic little
square, on the slopes of the Caelian Hills. It dates from 398,
when it was built by the Byzantine senator, on the site of the

house occupied by the Saints to whom it is dedicated. These, in the reign of Julian the Apostate of Terenziano, suffered martyrdom. Under the beautiful Romanesque bell-tower, are the ruins of the temple of Calusios. The portico and the outer gallery of the apse, are from the XII cent. — The three naved interior is not well-illuminated. In 1718, the church was restored. The rich chapel of Saint Paul of the Cross, the founder of the Passionist Order to whom the church belongs, is in the right nave. Of special interest are the *subterranean* portions of the building, with the important remains of the two-storied Roman house of the Martyrs, discovered in 1887. The decorations are fairly well-preserved: frieze, symbols, figures of saints, pagan motifs of the II-IV cent., and Christian moifs of the VII-VIII cent.

BATHS OF CARACALLA

Of the Baths of ancient Rome, they are second in magnitude only to the Baths of Diocletian. Constructed in 217 A. D. by the Emperor Caracalla, one of the most dissolute of the late Roman Emperiors, whose depraved way of life hastened the fall of the Empire, these Baths were used until VI cent. when they were devastated by the Gothic invaders. Rich in statues, stuccoes, and marbles, they were among the most beautiful and opulent structures of Rome. (In the National Museum, some of the objects found here, are exhibited). The first great hall, near the entrance, was the *Frigidarium*, where the swimming-pool was located. The *Tepidarium* is the center hall, which joined the court of the gymnasium. The *Calidarium* (vapour-bath) is a circular hall; measuring 35 meters in diameter. Adjacent to the Calidarium and around the gymnasium, were other halls used for sports, and other services. On summer evenings, operas are performed, among the ruins of the Calidarium.

Via di Porta San Sebastiano — It is a quaint, rather secluded street, enclosed by low walls. To the right, is the ancient, small church of *San Cesareo*, rich in beautiful Cosmatesque works

General view of the Baths of Caracalla.

of the XIII cent., and which also displays in the lower levels of
the building the mosaic floor of an ancient Bath of the II-II
cent. A.D. The church was restored in the XVI cent. Nearby, at
N. 8 is the *House of Cardinal Bessarione*, a gem of 15th cent.
architecture, surrounded by a garden, and furnished in the
style of the Renaissance. - Further on, at N. 9, is the entrance
to the *Tomb of the Scipios*, and the Columbarium of Pompo-
nius Hylas, which is the sepulchre of the family — Cornelius-
Scipione — a family which included many illustrious Romans
among whom is Scipio Africanus. A Roman house of the
Imperial period is above the sepulchre. An interesting visit is to
the Columbarium, with niches decorated with stuccoes and
paintings. At the end of the street is the Arch of Drusus, (circa
the II cent. A. D.). It once served as a support for the a-
queduct that supplied water for the Baths of Caracalla.

Porta San Sebastiano. — It was one of the 18 openings in
the Aurelian Wall, which was constructed between 271-78, and
in the V cent., reconstructed, by Belisarius. Two fine semi-cir-
cular, crenelated towers are on either side of the door. There
is a fine view from these towers.

Piazza della Navicella. — Named after the graceful 16th. cent. fountain in the center of this square, the *Fountain of the Navicella*. It is on the summit of the Caelian, the largest of the seven classic hills of Rome. Opposite, is the church of *Santa Maria in Domnica*. It is the oldest « diacona » (welfare center) of Rome. Over the centuries, it has been many times restored. On the triumphal arch, and in the apse, are important mosaics of the IX cent. - To the left of the church is the entrance to the public park of the *Villa Celimontana*. In the elegant 16th. cent. casino is the headquarters of the Geographic Society.

Church of SS. Quattro Coronati. — It is named after the four Roman legionaires who were martyred for refusing to worship Aesculapius, after they had been converted to Christianity. This impressive church, that dates from the IVth. cent., is remarkable for its surrounding walls, its massive bell-tower, and for the two atriums before the entrance. It gives the impression of strength. Reconstructed in the XII cent. it was subsequently many times restored. In the interior, of three naves and a women's gallery, there is a beautiful Cosmatesque pavement (XIII cent.); a 16th. cent. wooden ceiling, a gift of Cardinal Henry of Portugal, fragments of 14th. cent., frescoes, near the entrance, and in the left nave, frescoes in the animated style of Giovanni de San Giovanni (1630); and in the spacious apse, we see the Glory of the Saints. In the left nave, is the entrance to the exquisite Cosmatesque *Cloister*, one of the most beautiful works of the marble craftsmen of Rome (XII cent.). The elegant arcade is supported by gem-like double columns.

CHURCH OF SAN CLEMENTE

Dedicated to the Pope who was third in succession after Saint Peter, it is one of the better preserved mediaeval Roman churches. Originally built in the V cent., and destroyed by the Normans in 1084 it was reconstructed in 1108 by Paschal II, on the mound of the previous edifice. The original church had been built on ruins of the Imperial Period, and on an ancient Roman house of the Republican Period.

We enter the three-naved basilica from a side-door. The atrium, with its quadriportus is the only specimen of its kind in Rome (c. 1108). The naves are separated by 16 Roman columns;

SAN CLEMENTE. - To the left: « St. Catherine disputes before Maximian with the Doctors » and to the right: « St. Catherine liberated by an Angel », by Masolino da Panicale.

SAN CLEMENTE. - « Martyrdom of St. Clement », by Giovanni Odazzi.

the pavement is Cosmatesque. In the center is the beautiful Choir which had been in the lower Church. On the sides of the Choir are the Ambones, and a handsome Pascal candelabrum. The Presbytery is separated from the Choir by a screen of sculptured marble panels of the XII cent. (plutei and transenne). In the Presbyterium, which is above the crypt with the remains of Saint Clement, is the Tabernacle, supported by four noteworthy ancient columns of pavonnazzetto. In the apse is the magnificent mosaic of the Triumph of the Cross, of the Roman school of the XII cent., radiant with colour, and harmonius in composition. Here, the Crucifix, with 12 doves symbolizes the apostles above a multitude of persons. At the beginning of the left nave, is the famous *Chapel of Saint Catherine of Alexandria* adorned with the graceful frescoes of Masolino da Panicale (1431) c.), which portray: Scenes from the Lives of the Saint, and of Saint Ambrose; Crucifixion; Annunciation; Saint Christopher. From the Sacristy, we descend to the *Lower Church*. Crossing the vestibule, we come to the wide space of the ancient church, which had three naves. Here we see well-preserved frescoes of the VI to the XII cent. At the end of the left aisle are some ancient Roman stairs leading to a trench and several chambers of the Imperial Age. Following the ancient wall of the Republican Period, we reach a Chapel to Mithras, and the remains of a Roman house.

Santa Cecilia.

ELEVENTH ITINERARY

**Santa Cecilia in Trastevere - Santa Maria in Tra-
stevere - Farnesina - Gianicolo.**

CHURCH OF SANTA CECILIA IN TRASTEVERE

Founded in the V cent., on the site of the patron Saint,
it was rebuilt by Paschal I in the IX cent. The Saint had
appeared to him in a vision, and indicated where the
remains of her body were to be found in the Catacombs.
(Up to that time they were believed to be lost). The
tomb was found, just as had been indicated. This church
has been remodelled and redecorated several times. A
baroque door leads to a picturesque court, beyond which
is the baroque facade, with a mosaic frieze above
the portico, and a beautiful bell-tower of the XII cent.

Several important works of art are to be found in this church,
which has three-naves. At the side of the central door, two beautiful sepulchral monuments: to the right, the one dedicated to
Cardinal Hertford, by Paolo Romano (1398); to the left, the one
dedicated to Cardinal Forteguerri, by Mino da Fiesole (1437).
At the beginning of the right nave, a corridor, decorated by
P. Brill (1599) leads to the Calidarium of the Roman house
where Saint Cecilia suffered martyrdom, by being exposed
to the hot vapours. Above the altar, the Decapitation of the
Saint, of the school of Giulio Romano. The next chapel is
decorated with frescoes by Pintoricchio, and others. Above the

main altar is a fine tabernacle, by Arnolfo di Cambio (1283), and beneath the altar, an expressive statue of Saint Ceciila, by Stefano Maderno .It represents the body of the Saint in the exact position it was found, when the tomb was opened in 1559. In the tribune, precious mosaics depicting Christ and the Saints, of the IX cent.- From the Crypt, we may reach the remains of a Roman house, supposedly belonging to Saint Valerian, who was the husband of Saint Cecilia. In the adjoining convent, is a lovely cloister of the XIII cent., the choir of the nuns is decorated with an admirable fresco of the Last Judgment. This work is the masterpiece of P. Cavallini (end of XIII cent.).

Church of Santa Maria in Trastevere. — It is located in the square of the same name, which is embellished with a handsome 17th. cent. fountain, and where the *Palace of San Calisto* may also be seen. The first church was built by Julius I, in 340, on the site of the former oratory of St. Callixtus, founded in 222. This was the first large church in Rome dedicated to the Virgin. The present structure dates from 1130-43. On the facade, are mosaics of the XII-XIII cent. The bell-tower is Romanesque, the portico, beneath which we see fragments of inscriptions, was added by Carlo Fontana, in 1702. The interior is of three naves, separated by columns takes from ancient Roman temples; the pavement is Cosmatesque; the rich roof was designed by Domenichino, who also painted the Assumption (1617). In the tribune, and on the vault, exceptional mosaics depicting the Cross, the emblems of the Evangelists, and Christ and the Madonna enthroned among Saints, (1140). Lower down, the celebrated mosaics of Pietro Cavallini (1291) portraying episodes from the life of the Virgin, in six panels.

Piazza Trilussa. — It is at the beginning of Ponte Sisto, which was reconstructed by Baccio Ponticelli ,under Sixtus IV (1474). The beautiful 16th. cent. fountain, the so-called « Fontanone » was built from the designs of C. Fontana. On the left, crossing Via di Ponte Sisto and following Via Santa Dorotea, we come to N. 20, which is the famous *House of the Fornarina*. Here, according to tradition, lived the beloved of Raphael.

Palazzo Corsini. — It is at N. 10, Via della Lungara, and was constructed in the Baroque style, by Ferdinando Fuga, in 1732. The vestibule and the staircase are harmoniously designed. It is now the seat of the Accademia dei Lincei.

FARNESINA

This famous villa is one of the gems of Renaissance architecture. It was built by B. Peruzzi (1508-11) for Agostino Chigi, the famous Sienese banker, who was such an important figure in the financial circles of Europe, and of the Orient. He was also an enthusiastic patron of artists and writers, and this villa was the scene of many sumptuous banquets attended by popes, cardinals, princes and illustrious Italian and foreign personages. In 1580, the palace was transferred to the Farnese family. On the ground floor is the *Entrance-Hall*, with ceiling beautifully painted by Raphael (1517) with the help of Giulio Romano and others. It portrays the fable of Cupid and Psyche. In the next hall is the famous Galatea who is fleeing from the love of Polyphemus, by Raphael (1511), and on the ceiling, Constellations, by B. Peruzzi. Polyphemus and the scenes of the metamorphosis, are by Sebastiano del Piombo. On the first floor, the central hall is decorated with architectural paintings by B. Peruzzi, and others. In the bedroom, the Wedding of Alexander and Roxane, a fresco by Sodoma (1512).

Church of Sant'Onofrio. — Built in 1439, and subsequently many times redecorated, it rises at the top of a staircase, to the left of which is a terrace commanding a magnificent view. Below the portico, to the right, are three frescoes by Domenichino. - In the interior, in the first chapel to the left is the tomb of Torquato Tasso. Frescoes by Pintoricchio and Peruzzi (1503) adorn the polygonal apse. In the adjoining convent, which has a graceful cloister, Tasso lived the last years of his life, and here he died in 1595. In these room, there is now a small museum, with a collection of various personal objects of the poet, and some of his manuscripts.

The Janiculum.

GIANICOLO

It is the most popular road of Rome, and offers one of the most beautiful panoramas in the world. Having climbed the hill to San Onofrio, we come to the *Passeggiata del Gianicolo*. Continuing on this path, we find, midst a group of cypresses, *Tassos Oak* (blown down during a storm), in the shade of which the poet used to meditate. Rounding a wide curve, we come to the *Tower*, which is a symbol of Rome, and from here also, there is a fine view. Proceeding we come next to the monument to Anita Garibaldi, by M. Rutelli (1932), and the terrace of the Piazzale del Gianicolo, which is dominated by the equestrian statue of Giuseppe Garibaldi, by E. Gallori (1895). The view here is truly magnificent. Opposite the piazzale, the road, flanked by busts of patriots of the Roman Republic (1849), leads to the exit of the Gianicolo. To the right of the exit is the monumental *Fontana dell'Acqua Paola;* a fountain built in 1612, by G. Fontana, and C. Maderno ,commissioned by Paul V.

San Pietro in Montorio. — It rises on the site where according to an ancient tradition, Saint Peter was believed to have been crucified. The present facade, in simple Renaissance style, dates from the XV cent. - Within the church, which consists of one nave with chapels, there are many noteworthy works of art, including the world famous Flagellation of Christ, and other frescoes by Sebastiano del Piombo, in the first chapel to the right. In the second chapel, the Incoronation of Mary, and the Four Virtues, by B. Peruzzi. The work of Dirck van Baburen, in the Caravaggio manner, is in the fourth chapel to the left (1617). In the adjacent court which we may enter from the right side of the church, the celebrated *Temple of Bramante,* the is first work executed by the artist in Rome (1502). This round domed building is considered to be one of the most elegant buildings of modern times.

GIANICOLO. - Monument to Giuseppe Garibaldi.

The Old Appian Way.

TWELFTH ITINERARY

Via Appia Antica - Domine Quo Vadis? - The Catacombs of Saint Callixtus - San Sebastiano - Tomb of Caecilia Metella - Ancient Zone of the Appian Way.

VIA APPIA ANTICA

It is the most celebrated Roman road, and is also known as the *Regina viarum*. It was begun by Appius Claudius Caecus, the Censor, in 312 B. C., and the great modern highway we see today was built on the same site. The road preserves its original character, and the principal monuments have been restored. It is of great interest historically. Originally the chief line of communication between Rome and Southern Italy, Greece, the Eastern possessions of the Roman Empire etc., along its sides at *Porta San Sebastiano* and winds along a picturesque route if the country.

Domine Quo Vadis ? — It rises on the site where, according to the legend, the vision of Christ appeared to the Apostle Peter, counseling him to return to Rome, which he had fled, in order to escape presecution and martyrdom. « Domine quo vadis » (« Lord, where are you going? » asked Peter). « Venio iterum crucifigi » (« I am going to be crucified a second time ») answered Christ. Then Peter turned back to Rome ando to martyrdom. Within the little church (rebuilt in 1600) is a marble-slab bearing, according to legend, the foot-marks which Christ is said to have left on the pavement. The original is preserved at San Sebastiano.

VIA APPIA ANTICA. - To the left: **Church of the « Domine Quo Vadis? »**; to the right: **Tomb of Cecilia Metella.**

THE CATACOMBS OF SAINT CALLIXTUS

These are the most important catacombs of Rome. They date from the II cent. Originally, an ancient Roman necropoli, they were used by the Early Christians as a meeting-place, and as a place of worship, as well as a haven from the persecution. From the small church, at the end of a cypress-lined path, accompanied by a guide, we descend into the Catacombs to visit the Crypt of the Popes (III cent.); the crypt where the venerated tomb of Saint Cecilia since restored (discovered by Paschal I (812)), with frescoes on the VII-VIII cent., five little cells of the Sacraments, with frescoes of the III cent. and the crypt of Pope Eusebius (309).

SAN SEBASTIANO

Built in the IV cent., to honour the memory of the martyred Saint next to the cemetery where the Apostles Peter and Paul were first buried. Rebuilt in the XVII cent., the facade with portico is by G. Vasanzio, who also designed the wooden ceiling of the church. In the first chapel to the left is the stone with the foot-prints left by Christ on the Via Appia when he was met by St. Peter who was fleeing from Rome. In the chapel opposite, the statue of Saint Sebastian, by A. Giorgetti (XVII cent.).

From a small museum, which we enter from the atrium of the church, we may descend to the *catacombs*. They are of exceptional historical interest, and arranged in four tiers. In the second gallery we find the Crypt of Saint Sebastian. Here too are many inscriptions left by the Early Christians with allegories of animals, each one of symbolical importance.

The Circus of Maxentius. — About 300 meters beyond San Sebastiano, to the left, are the ruins of the Circus of Maxentius,

Catacombs of St. Callixtus.

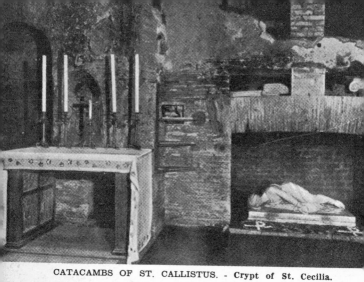

CATACAMBS OF ST. CALLISTUS. - Crypt of St. Cecilia.

CATACOMBS OF ST. CALLIXTUS. - Crypt of the Popes.

one of the most perfectly conserved monuments of antiquity. It was erected by the Emperor in 309, in honour of his son Romulus, whose tomb is near-by.

TOMB OF CAECILIA METELLA

It is the most famous monument on the Appian Way. It dates from the last years of the Republic, and was originally the tomb of Caecilia Metella, the daughter of Quintus Metellus Creticus, and the wife of one of the sons of the Triumvirate Crassus, according to the inscription near the road. It is a cylindrical tower (20 meters in diameter), covered with travertine, and, above, decorated with a beautiful frieze representing Gallic shields, and ram's heads. In 1302 the Caetani transformed the monument into a stronghold of their family. From this period are the battlements.

ANCIENT ZONE OF THE APPIAN WAY

A short distance away from the tomb of Caecilia Metella, begins the ancient thoroughfare. Along the side, against a background of the vast and peaceful landscape of the Roman Campagna, are the ruins of small tombs. Here the street is no longer paved with asphalt, instead, we see the famous ancient Roman pavement, in « opus incertum ». Noteworthy among the many tombs are the *Mounds of the Horatii and Curiatii* in the archaic style, supposedly the burial place of the heroes who were killed in the legendary duel. Next, are the great ruins of the *Villa of the Quintilii*, that once belonged to the brothers Quintilii, They were assassinated by Emperor Commodus in 182 so that the could possess himself of their property. Seven kilometers down the road, is the interesting *Casale Rotondo*, a large round tomb on a square base, from the Augustan Period.

Catacombe of Domitilla. — The entrance is at N. 282, Via delle Sette Chiese. The most extensive of Rome, they were built at the end of the 1st. cent. by Saint Domitilla, the niece of Emperor Domitian. Most interesting is the visit to the church built in the IV cent. over the tombs of SS. Nereus and Achilleus; the underground chamber of the Flavians, with decorations of the 1st. cent. A.D.; and the cell of Saint Petronilla.

CATACOMBS OF ST. CALLIXTUS. - Sarcophagus with biblical scenes.
(IV cent.).

AN IMPORTANT NEW
ARCHAEOLOGICAL DISCOVERY

Very recently, on February 5th 1964, an important archaeological discovery was made in Rome. On the via Cassia, eleven kilometres from Rome, near the crossing of Grottarossa, a sarcophagus containing a mummy was found during excavations for the construction of a new building; the first such discovery in Italy and, most probably also the last one. The process of embalment practised in the Orient was a technique unknown to the Latin world. For this reason the archaeologists are still uncertain of the origin and nationality of the mummy. Its age has been determined by anatomical examinations as being about eight years, and is of a girl presumabely belonging to a Roman family who died about 160 A. D.. When found, it was wrapped in linen-strips from which still intensely emanated the acute aroma of the resins used for conservation. Various objects of gold decorated the minute body, about 1,20 m long: two little rings at the lobes of the ears, a chain of losanges alternating with blue glass-beads and a ring on which is engraved a winged Victory with crown and torch. Other objects belonging to the deceased that

Sarcophagus with episodes of the hunt, in which was discovered the mummy of the young girl called «Giustinianella» (the name refers to the place where the mummy was first brought).

The body of the « Giustinianella ».

were found beside the body, were a broken ebony-doll, a vase for balsam in the form of a shell and three small vases of various shapes. The sarcophagus in which was found the mummy called « Giustinianella » (so called after the place where it was first taken), was surrounded by valuable sculptures unfortunately partially damaged during the excavation. The sarcophagus originally was of white marble, but time had given it a rose patina. It is delicately sculptured on three sides with hunting scenes. Of particular interest is the fact, that in contrast to other sarcophagi the hunting-scene begins and ends on the short sides, while on the long side is carved a horseman with a Phrygian berret. After discovery the mummy was taken to the Museo delle Terme and is exhibited to the public in a glass-urn at the side of the sarcophagus in which it was protected from decay for eighteen centuries.

THE ROMAN CAMPAGNA. - The ruins of the aqueduct of Claudius.

EXCAVATIONS AT OSTIA. - The ruins of an ancient Synagogue discovered in 1961.

Giorni di visita e orario delle
GALLERIE, MUSEI E MONUMENTI

Days of visit and time-table of
GALLERIES, MUSEUMS AND MONUMENTS

Jours de visite et horaires des
GALERIES, DES MUSÉES ET DES MONUMENTS

Besuchstage und Oeffnungszeiten der
GALLERIEN, MUSEEN UND DENKMAELER

ARA PACIS AUGUSTAE. - Via di Ripetta.
Dalle ore 9 alle 16. Giorni festivi dalle ore 9 alle 13. Il lunedì chiusa.

ARA PACIS AUGUSTAE. - Via di Ripetta.
Weekdays 9 a.m. 4 p.m. Sundays and holidays 9 a.m. 1 p.m. Closed on Mondays.

ARA PACIS AUGUSTAE. - Via di Ripetta.
En semaine de 9h. à 16h. Les jours fériés: de 9h. à 13h. Fermée le lundi.

ARA PACIS AUGUSTAE. - Via di Ripetta.
Von 9 bis 16 Uhr. An Festtagen von 9 bis 13 Uhr. Montags geschlossen.

CARCERE MAMERTINO. - Via del Foro Romano.
Dalle ore 8 alle 12.30 e dalle ore 14 al tramonto

CARCERE MAMERTINO. - Via del Foro Romano.
Open daily 8 a.m. 12.30 a.m. - 3 p.m. till sunset.

PRISON MAMERTINE. - Via del Foro Romano.
De 8h. à 12h. 30 et de 14h. au coucher du soleil.

CARCERE MAMERTINO. - Via del Foro Romano.
Von 8 bis 12.30 Uhr und von 14 Uhr bis Sonnenuntergang.

CATACOMBE DI PRISCILLA. - Via Salaria, 430.
Dalle ore 9 alle 12 e dalle ore 15 al tramonto.

CATACOMBS OF PRISCILLA. - Via Salaria, 430.
Open daily 9 a.m. 12 a.m. and from 3 p.m. till sunset.

CATACOMBES DE PRISCILLE. - Via Salaria, 430.
De 9h. à midi et de 15h. au coucher du soleil.

CATAKOMBEN VON PRISCILLA. - Via Salaria, 430.
Von 9 bis 12 Uhr und von 15 Uhr bis Sonnenuntergang.

CATACOMBE DI S. AGNESE. - Sotto la chiesa dello stesso nome e in via Nomentana.
Dalle ore 8 alle 12 e dalle ore 15 al tramonto.

CATACOMBS OF ST. AGNESE. - Under the Church of same name, via Nomentana.
Open daily 8 a.m. 12 a.m. - from 3 p.m. till sunset.

CATACOMBES DE STE. AGNES. - Au-dessous de l'église ho
monyme à la Via Nomentana, 349.
De 8h. à midi et de 15h. au coucher du soleil.

KATAKOMBEN VON ST. AGNESE. - Unterhalb der Kirche
gleichen Namens, und in via Nomentana.
Von 8 bis 12 Uhr und von 15 Uhr bis Sonnenuntergang.

CATACOMBE DI S. CALLISTO. - Via Appia Antica, 102-110 c
via Ardeatina, 171.
Dalle ore 8 alle 12 e dalle ore 15 al tramonto.

CATACOMBS OF ST. CALLIXTUS. - Via Appia Antica, 102-110
Via Ardeatina 171.
Open daily 8 a.m. 12 a.m. - from 3 p.m. till sunset.

CATACOMBES DE ST. CALIXTE. - Via Appia Antica, 102-110
ou Via Ardeatina, 171.
De 8h. à midi et de 15h. au coucher du soleil.

KATAKOMBEN VON ST. CALIXTUS. - Via Appia Antica, 102-
110 oder via Ardeatina, 171.
Von 8 bis 12 Uhr und von 15 Uhr bis Sonnenuntergang.

CATACOMBE DI S. DOMITILLA. - Via delle Sette Chiese, 282
Dalle ore 8.30 alle 12 e dalle ore 15 al tramonto.

CATACOMBS OF ST. DOMITILLA. - Via delle Sette Chiese, 282
Open daily 8.30 a.m. 12 a.m. - from 3 p.m. till sunset.

CATACOMBES DE STE. DOMITIE. - Via delle Sette Chiese
282.
De 8h. à midi et de 14h. 30 au coucher du soleil.

KATAKOMBEN VON ST. DOMITILLA. - Via delle Sette Chie
se, 282.
Von 8.30 bis 12 Uhr und von 15 Uhr bis Sonnenuntergang

CATACOMBE DI S. SEBASTIANO. - Via Appia Antica, 182.
Dalle ore 8.30 alle 12 e dalle ore 15 al tramonto.

CATACOMBS OF ST. SEBASTIAN. - Via Appia Antica, 182.
Open daily 8.30 a.m. 12 a.m. - from 3 p.m. till sunset.

CATACOMBES DE ST. SÉBASTIEN. - Via Appia Antica, 132
De 8h. 30 à midi et de 15h. au coucher du soleil.

KATAKOMBEN VON ST. SEBASTIAN. - Via Appia Antica, 182
Von 8.30 bis 12 Uhr und von 15 Uhr bis Sonnenuntergang

COLOSSEO (Visita alle Gallerie superiori).
   Dalle ore 9 ad un'ora prima' del tramonto.
COLOSSEUM (Visit to the upper Galleries).
   From 9 a.m. till an hour before sunset.
COLISÉE (Visite aux galeries supérieures)
   De 9h. à une heure avant le coucher du soleil.
COLOSSEUM (Besuchszeiten für die oberen Gallerien).
   Von 9 Uhr bis eine Stunde vor Sonnenuntergang.

CUPOLA DI S. PIETRO. - Basilica di San Pietro.
   Dalle ore 8.15 ad un'ora e 30 minuti prima dell'Ave Maria
CUPOLA DI S. PIETRO. - Basilica of St. Peter's.
   Open from 8.15 a.m. till an hour and 30 minutes before the
   « Ave Maria ».
COUPOLE DE SAINT PIERRE. - Basilique de St. Pierre.
   De 8h. 15 à une heure et demi environ avant l'Angélus du
   soir.
KUPPEL VON ST. PETER. - Basilika von St. Peter.
   Von 8.15 Uhr bis 90 Minuten vor dem Ave Maria.

DOMUS AUREA. - Via Labicana, 136 (Colle Oppio).
   Dalle ore 9 ad un'ora prima del tramonto.
DOMUS AUREA. - Via Labicana, 136 (Colle Oppio).
   From 9 a.m. till an hour before sunset.
DOMUS AUREA. - Via Labicana, 136 (Colle Oppio).
   De 9h. à une heure avant le coucher du soleil.
DOMUS AUREA. - Via Labicana, 136 (Oppio-Hügel).
   Von 9 Uhr bis eine Stunde vor Sonnenuntergang.

FARNESINA. - Via della Lungara, 230.
   Dalle ore 10 alle 13. La domenica chiusa.
FARNESINA. - Via della Lungara, 230.
   From 10 a.m. till 1 p.m. Closed on Sundays.
FARNESINA. - Via della Lungara, 230.
   De 10h. à 13h. Fermé le dimanche.
FARNESINA. - Via della Lungara, 230.
   Von 10 bis 13 Uhr. Sonntags geschlossen.

FORO DI AUGUSTO. - Via Campo Carleo.
   Ottobre-Maggio dalle ore 10 alle 17. Giugno-Settembre dal
   le ore 9 alle 13 e dalle 15 alle 18. Giorni festivi dalle 9 alle
   13. Il lunedì chiuso.
FORUM OF AUGUSTUS. - Via Campo Carleo.
   October-May 10 a.m. 15 p.m. June-September 9 a.m. 1 p.m
   and 3 p.m. 6 p.m. Holydays 9 a.m. 1 p.m. Closed on Mondays
FORUM D'AUGUSTE. - Via Campo Carleo.
   D'October à Mai de 10 h. à 17 h.. de Juin à September de
   9h. à 13h. et de 15h. à 18h. Les jours fériés, de 9h. à 13h
   Fermé le lundi.
FORUM AUGUSTUS. - Via Campocarleo.
   Oktober bis Mai von 10 bis 17 Uhr. Juni bis September
   von 9 bis 13 und 15 bis 18 Uhr. An Feiertagen von 9 bis 13
   Uhr. Montags geschlossen.

FORO DI CESARE. - Clivo Argentario.
   Ottobre-Maggio dalle ore 10 alle 17. Giugno-Settembre dalle
   ore 9 alle 13 e dalle 15 alle 18. Il lunedì chiuso.
FORUM OF CAESAR. - Clivo Argentario.
   October-May 10 a.m. 5 p.m. June-September 9 a.m. 1 p.m
   and 3 p.m. 6 p.m. Closed on Mondays
FORUM DE CÉSAR. Clivus Argentaire.
   D'October à Mai de 10h. à 17h.; de Juin à September de
   9h. à 13h. et de 15h. à 18h. Fermé le lundi.
FORUM CAESAR. - Clivo Argentario.
   Oktober bis Mai von 10 bis 17 Uhr. Juni bis September von
   9 bis 13 und 15 bis 18 Uhr. Montags geschlossen.

FORO ROMANO E PALATINO. - Via dei Fori Imperiali e
   Via San Gregorio.
   Dalle ore 9 ad un'ora prima del tramonto.
ROMAN AND PALATINE FORUM. - Via dei Fori Imperiali;
   via San Gregorio.
   Open daily from 9 a.m. till an hour before sunset.
FORUM ROMAIN ET PALATIN. Via dei Fori Imperiali et
   Via S. Gregorio.
   De 9 h. une heure avant le coucher du soleil.

FORUM ROMANUM UND PALATIN. - Via dei Fori Imperiali
und Via San Gregorio.
Von 9 Uhr bis eine Stunde vor Sonnenuntergang.

FORO DI TRAJANO. - Piazza del Foro Trajano.
Ottobre-Maggio dalle ore 10 alle 17. Giugno-Settembre dalle
ore 9 alle 13 e dalle ore 15 alle 18. Il lunedì chiuso.

FORUM OF TRAJAN. - Piazza del Foro di Trajano.
October-May 10 a.m. 5 p.m. June-September 9 a.m. 1 p.m. -
3 p.m. 6 p.m. Closed on Mondays.

FORUM DE TRAJAN. - Place du Forum de Trajan.
D'Octobre à Mai de 10h. à 17h. De Juin à September de
9h. à 13h. et de 15h. à 18h. Fermé le Lundi.

FORUM DES TRAJAN. - Piazza del Foro Trajano.
Oktober bis Mai von 10 bis 17 Uhr. Juni bis September von
9 bis 13 und 15 bis 18 Uhr. Montags geschlossen.

GALLERIA BORGHESE. - Villa Umberto, 1.
Novembre-Maggio dalle ore 9.30 alle 16. Giugno-Ottobre dalle ore 9 alle 13 e dalle ore 16 alle 18. In Luglio e Agosto
anche dalle ore 21 alle 23.30.

GALLERIA BORGHESE. - Villa Umberto, 1.
November-May 9.30 a.m. 4 p.m. - June-September 9 a.m.
1 p.m. - 4 p.m. 6 p.m. In July and August also from 9 p.m.
till 11.30 p.m.

GALERIE BORGHESE. - Villa Umberto, 1.
De Novembre à Mai de 9h. 30 à 16h. De Juin à Octobre
de 9h. à 13h et de 16h. à 18h. En Juillet et Août aussi de 21h.
à 23h. 30.

GALLERIA BORGHESE. - Villa Umberto, 1.
November bis Mai von 9.30 bis 16 Uhr. Juni bis Oktober
von 9 bis 13 und 16 bis 18 Uhr. Im Juli und August auch
von 21 bis 23.30 Uhr.

GALLERIA COLONNA. - Via della Pilotta, 17.
Aperta ai visitatori solo il sabato dalle ore 9 alle 13.

GALLERIA COLONNA. - Via della Pilotta, 17.
Open to the visitors every Saturday 9 a.m. - 1 p.m.

GALERIE COLONNA. - Via della Pilotta, 17.
Ouverte seulement le Samedi de 9h. à 13h.
GALLERIA COLONNA. - 'Via della Pilotta, 17.
Für Besucher nur am Samstag von 9 bis 13 Uhr geöffnet.

GALLERIA CORSINI. - Via della Lungara, 10.
Aperta dalle ore 9 alle 13.
GALLERIA CORSINI. - Via della Lungara, 10.
Open daily 9 a.m. - 1 p.m.
GALERIE CORSINI. - Via della Lungara, 10.
Ouverte de 9h. à 13h.
GALLERIA CORSINI. - Via della Lungara, 10.
Geöffnet von 9 bis 13 Uhr.

GALLERIA DORIA-PAMPHILJ. - Piazza del Collegio Romano, 2.
Aperta il martedì, venerdì, sabato e domenica dalle ore alle
13.
GALLERIA DORIA-PAMPHILJ. - Piazza del Collegio Romano, 2.
Open Tuesdays, Fridays, Saturdays and Sundays 10 a.m. -
1 p.m.
GALERIE DORIA- PAMPHILJ. - Place del Collegio Romano, 2.
Ouverte Mardi, Vendredi, Samedi et Dimanche de 10h. à
13h.
GALLERIA DORIA-PAMPHILJ. - Piazza del Collegio Romano, 2.
Geöffnet Dienstags, Freitags; Samstags und Sonntags von
10 bis 13 Uhr.

GALLERIA NAZIONALE D'ARTE ANTICA. - (Pal. Barberini)
Via Quattro Fontane, 13.
Novembre-Maggio dalle ore 9,30 alle 16. Giugno-Ottobre
dalle ore 9 alle 13 e dalle ore 15.30 alle 18. Mesi estivi il
mercoledì anche dalle ore 21 alle 23.30.
GALLERIA NAZIONALE D'ARTE ANTICA. - (Pal. Barberini)
Via Quattro Fontane, 13.
November-May 9.30 a.m. 4 p.m. June-October 9 a.m. 1 p.m.
3.30 p.m. 6 p.m. During summer months on Wednesdays also
from 9 p.m. till 11.30 p.m.

GALERIE NATIONALE D'ART ANCIEN. - (Pal. Barberini) Via
Quattro Fontane, 13.
De Novembre à Mai de 9h. 30 16h. De Juin à Octobre de
9h. à 13h. et de 15h. 30 à 18h. En été le Mercredi de 21h. à
23h. 30.

NATIONAL GALLERIE FUER ANTIKE KUNST. - (Pal. Barberini) Via Quattro Fontane, 13.
November bis Mai von 9.30 bis 16 Uhr. Juni bis Oktober
von 9 bis 13 und 15.30 bis 18 Uhr. In den Sommermonaten
am Mittwoch auch von 21 bis 23.30 Uhr.

GALLERIA NAZIONALE D'ARTE MODERNA. - Via delle Belle
Arti, 135 (Valle Giulia).
Ottobre-Maggio dalle ore 9.30 alle 16. Giugno-Settembre
dalle ore 9.30 alle 13 e dalle ore 15 alle 18. Durante i mesi
estivi il venerdì anche dalle ore 21,30 alle 23.30. Il lunedì
chiusa.

GALLERIA NAZIONALE D'ARTE MODERNA. - Via delle Belle
Arti, 135 (Valle Giulia).
October-May 9.30 a.m. 4 p.m. June-September 9.30 a.m. -
1 p.m. - 3 p.m. 6 p.m. During summer months on Fridays
also from 9.30 p.m. till 11.30 p.m. Closed on Mondays.

GALERIE NATIONALE D'ART MODERNE. - Viale delle Belle
Arti, 135 (Valle Giulia).
D'Octobre à Mai de 9h. 30 à 16h. De Juin à Septembre de
9h. 30 à 12h. et de 15h. à 18h. Fermé le lundi, en été le
vendreri de 21h. 30 à 23h. 30.

NATIONALGALLERIE FUER MODERNE KUNST. - Via delle
Belle Arti 135 (Valle Giulia).
Oktober bis Mai von 9.30 bis 16 Uhr. Juni bis September
von 9.30 bis 13 und 15 bis 18 Uhr. Während der Sommermonate Freitags auch von 21.30 bis 23.30. Montags geschlossen.

GIARDINO ZOOLOGICO. - Villa Borghese.
Dalle ore 8.30 fino al tramonto.

ZOOLOGICAL GARDEN. - Villa Borghese.
8.30 a.m. till sunset.

JARDIN ZOOLOGIQUE. - Villa Borghese.
De 8h. 30 au coucher du soleil.

ZOOLOGISCHER GARTEN. - Villa Borghese.
Von 8.30 bis Sonnenuntergang.

GROTTE VATICANE. - Basilica di S. Pietro.
Dalle ore 8.15 alle 13 e dalle ore 14.30 ad un'ora e 30 minuti prima dell'Ave Maria.

GROTTE VATICANE (Vatican Caves). - Basilica of St. Peter's.
8.15 a.m. 1 p.m. ⊢ 2.30 p.m. till an hour and 30 minutes before the « Ave Maria ».

GROTTES VATICANES. - Basilique de St. Pierre.
De 8h. 15 à 13h. et de 14h. 30 à une heure et demi environ avant l'Angélus du soir.

VATIKANGROTTEN. - Basilica von St. Peter.
Von 8.15 bis 13 und 14.30 Uhr bis 1 Stunde und 30 Min. vor dem Ave Maria.

MERCATI TRAJANEI. - Via IV Novembre 94 - piazza del Foro Trajano.
Ottobre-Maggio dalle ore 10 alle 17. Giugno-Settembre dalle ore 9 alle 13 e dalle ore 15 alle 18. Il lunedì chiusi.

TRAJAN MARKETS. - Via IV Novembre, 94 - Piazza del Foro Trajano.
October-May 10 a.m. 5 p.m. June-September 9 a.m. 1 p.m. - 3 p.m. 6 p.m. Closed on Mondays.

LES MARCHÉS DE TRAJAN. - Via IV Novembre, 94 et Place du Forum de Trajan.
D'Octobre à Mai de 10h. à 17h. De Juin à Septembre de 9h. à 13h. et de 15h. à 18h. Fermé le lundi.

TRAJANSMAERKTE. - Via IV Novembre 94. - Piazza del Forum Trajano.
Oktober bis Mai von 10 bis 17 Uhr. Juni bis September von 9 bis 13 und 15 bis 18 Uhr. Montags geschlossen.

MUSEI CAPITOLINI. - Piazza del Campidoglio.
Dalle ore 9 alle 16. Il sabato anche dalle ore 21 alle 23.30. Festivi dalle ore 9 alle 13. Il lunedì chiusi.

MUSEI CAPITOLINI. - Piazza del Campidoglio.
9 a.m. 4 p.m. On Saturdays also from 9 p.m. till 11.30 p.m. Holidays 9 a.m. 1 p.m. Closed on Mondays.

MUSÉES CAPITOLINS. - Place du Capitole.
De 9h. à 16h. Le Samedi de 21h. à 23h. 30. Les jours fériés de 9h. à 13h. Fermés le lundi.

KAPITOLINISCHE MUSEEN. Piazza del Campidoglio.
Von 9 bis 16 Uhr. Samstags auch von 21 bis 23.30 Uhr. An Feiertagen von 9 bis 13 Uhr. Montags geschlossen.

MUSEI E GALLERIE PONTIFICE. - Viale Vaticano.
Dalle ore 9 alle 14. La domenica chiusi.

MUSEUMS AND GALLERIES OF THE VATICAN CITY. - Viale Vaticano.
9 a.m. 2 p.m. Closed on Sundays.

MUSÉES ET GALERIES DU VATICAN. - Viale Vaticano
De 9h. à 14h. Fermés le Dimanche.

PAEPSTLICHE MUSEEN UND GALLERIEN. - Viale Vatikano
Von 9 bis 14 Uhr. Sonntags geschlossen.

MUSEI LATERANENSI. - Piazza di Porta San Giovanni.
Musei Profano e Cristiano: on Mondays, Wednesdays, Friore 9 alle 14. Museo Missionario Etnologico: martedì, giovedì, sabato dalle ore 9 alle 14.

LATERAN MUSEUMS. - Piazza di Porta San Giovanni.
Musei Profano e Cristiano: on Mondays, Wednesday, Fridays 9 a.m. 2 p.m. Museo Missionario Etnologico: on Tuesdays. Thursdays, Saturdays 9 a.m. 2 p.m.

MUSÉES DE LATRAN. - Place de la Porte St. Jean.
Musée profane et Chrétien, Lundi, mercredi et vendredi de 9h. à 14h. Musée ethnoligique des mission: mardi, jeudi et samedi de 9 h. à 14 h.

LATERANENSISCHE MUSEEN. - Piazza di Porta San Giovanni.
Profane und christliche Museen: Montags, Mittwochs, Freitags von 9 bis 14 Uhr. Ethnologisches Missionarmuseum: Dienstags, Donnerstags, Samstags von 9 bis 14 Uhr.

MUSEO DELLA CIVILTA' ROMANA. - Piazza Agnelli (E.U.R.).
Ottobre-Maggio dalle ore 9 alle 14. Giugno-Settembre dalle ore 16 alle 20. Rimane chiuso il lunedì e nel mese di Agosto.

227

MUSEO DELLA CIVILTA' ROMANA. - Piazza Agnelli (E.U.R.).
October-May 9 a.m. 2 p.m. June-September 4 p.m. 8 p.m.
Closed on Mondays and in August.

MUSÉE DE LA CIVILISATION ROMAINE. - Place Agnelli
(E.U.R.).
D'Octobre à Mai de 9h. à 14h. De Juin à Septembre de
16h. à 20h. Fermé le lundi et durant le mois d'août.

ROEMISCHES BUERGERMUSEUM. - Piazza Agnelli (E.U.R.).
Oktober bis Mai von 9 bis 14 Uhr. Juni bis September
von 16 bis 20 Uhr. Jeden Montag und während des Monats
August geschlossen.

MUSEO NAZIONALE ROMANO O DELLE TERME. - Via delle
Terme.
Novembre-Maggio dalle ore 9.30 alle 16. Giugno-Ottobre
dalle ore 9.30 alle 18. Durante i mesi estivi il martedì anche
dalle ore 21 alle 23.30. Il lunedì chiuso.

MUSEO NAZIONALE ROMANO OR DELLE TERME. - Via delle
Terme.
November-May 9.30 a.m. 4 p.m. June-October 9.30 a.m. 6 p.m.
In summer months on tuesdays also from 9 p.m. till 11.30
p.m. Closed on Mondays.

MUSÉE NATIONAL ROMAIN OU DES THERMES. - Via delle
Terme.
De Novembre à Mai de 9h. 30 à 16h. De Juin à Octobre de
9h. 30 à 18h. En été le mardi aussi de 21h. à 23h. 30. Fermé
le lundi.

ROEMISCHES NATIONALMUSEUM ODER THERMENMUSEUM
Via delle Terme.
November bis Mai von 9.30 bis 16 Uhr. Juni bis Oktober
von 9.30 bis 18 Uhr. Während der Sommermonate Dienstags auch von 21 bis 23.30 Uhr.

MUSEO NAZIONALE DI VILLA GIULIA. - Piazza di Villa
Giulia, 9.
Ottobre-Maggio dalle ore 9 alle 15 (festivi dalle ore 9.30
alle 13.30). Giugno-Settembre dalle ore 9 alle 16 (festivi dalle
ore 9 alle 13). Durante i mesi estivi il sabato anche dalle
ore 21 alle 23.30. Il lunedì chiuso.

NATIONAL MUSEUM OF VILLA GIULIA. - Piazza di Villa
Giulia, 9.
October-May 9 a.m. 3 p.m. (holidays 9.30 a.m. 1.30 p.m.)
June-September 9 a.m. 4 p.m. (holidays 9 a.m. 1 p.m.).
During summer months on Saturdays also 8 p.m. 11.30 p.m.
Closed on Mondays.

MUSÉE NATIONAL DE VILLA JULIE. - Piazzale de Villa
Julie, 9.
D'Octobre à Mai de 9h. à 15h. (fériés de 9h. 30 à 13h. 30).
De Juin à September de 9h. à 16h. (feriés de 9h. à 13h.). En
été le samedi aussi de 21h. à 23h. 30. Fermé le lundi.

NATIONALMUSEUM VILLA GIULIA. - Piazza di Villa Giulia 9.
Oktober mis Mai von 9 bis 15 Uhr (an Feiertagen von 9.30
bis 13.30). Juni bis September von 9 bis 16 Uhr (an Feiertagen von 9 bis 13 Uhr). Während der Sommermonate
Samstags auch von 21 bis 23.30. Montags geschlossen.

MUSEO DI PALAZZO VENEZIA. - Piazza Venezia, 3.
Novembre-Aprile dalle ore 9.30 alle 16 (domenica dalle ore
9.30 alle 17). Maggio-Ottobre dalle ore 9 alle 13 e dalle ore
15.30 alle 18 (la domenica e festivi infrasettimanali dalle ore
9 alle 13.30). Il lunedì chiuso.

MUSEUM OF PALAZZO VENEZIA. - Piazza Venezia, 3.
November-April 9.30 a.m. 4 p.m. (Sundays 9.30 a.m. 5 p.m.)
May-October 9 a.m. 1 p.m. - 3.30 p.m. 6 p.m. (Sundays and
holidays 9 a.m. 1.30 p.m.). Closed on Mondays.

MUSÉE DU PALAIS DE VENISE. - Place de Venise, 3.
De Novembre à Avril de 9h. 30 à 16h. Ie Dimanche de
9h. 30 à 17h. De Mai à Octobre de 9h à 13h. et de 15.30 à
18h. Les jours fériés de 9h. à 13h. 30. Fermé le lundi.

MUSEUM PALAZZO VENEZIA. - Piazza Venezia, 3.
November bis April von 9.30 bis 16 Uhr (Sonntags von 9.30
bis 17 Uhr). Mai bis Oktober von 9 bis 13 und 15.30 bis 18
Uhr. (An Sonn- und Feiertagen während der Woche von
9 bis 13.30). Montags geschlossen.

MUSEO DI ROMA. - Piazza di S. Pantaleo, 10 (Pal. Braschi).
Dalle ore 9 alle 14. Festivi dalle ore 9 alle 13. Il lunedì
chiuso.

MUSEO DI ROMA. - Piazza di S. Pantaleo, 10 (Pal. Braschi).
9 a.m. 2 p.m. on Holidays 9 a.m. 1 p.m. Closed on Mondays.

MUSÉE DE ROME. - Place de S. Pantaleo, 10 (Palais Braschi).
De 9h. à 14h. Jours fériés de 9h. à 13h. Fermé le lundi.

ROM-MUSEUM - Piazza di San Pantaleo, 10 (Pal. Braschi).
Von 9 bis 14 Uhr. An Feiertagen von 9 bis 13 Uhr. Montags geschlossen.

PALAZZO FARNESE. - Piazza Farnese.
Domenica dalle ore 11 alle 12.

PALAZZO FARNESE. - Piazza Farnese.
On Sundays 11 a.m. 12 p.m.

PALAIS FARNESE. - Place Farnèse.
Dimanche de 11h. à 12h.

PALAZZO FARNESE. - Piazza Farnese.
Sonntags von 11 bis 12 Uhr.

PALAZZO DEL QUIRINALE. - Piazza del Quirinale.
Aperto tutti i giovedì. 1º Ottobre 30 Aprile dalle ore 14 alle 16.30. Dal 1º Maggio al 30 Settembre dalle ore 13 alle 17.30. Per l'accesso è necessario un documento d'identità.

PALAZZO DEL QUIRINALE. - Piazza del Quirinale.
Open every Thursday. From October 1st. till April 30th 2 p.m. 4.30 p.m. From May 1st. till September 30th 1 p.m. 5.30 p.m. Identity cards or passaport must be shown.

PALAIS DU QUIRINAL. - Place du Quirinal.
Ouvert tous les Jeudi. Du 1º Octobre au 30 Avril de 14h. à 16h. 30. Du 1º Mai au 30 Septembre de 13h. à 17h. 30 Pour le visiter on doit avoir sa carte d'identité.

PALAST DES QUIRINAL. - Piazza del Quirinale.
Jeden Donnerstag geöffnet. 1. Oktober bis 30. April von 14 bis 16.30 Uhr. Vom 1. Mai bis 30. September von 13 bis 17.30 Uhr. Für den Eintritt ist ein Personalausweis nötig.

TERME DI CARACALLA. - Via delle Terme di Caracalla.
Dalle ore 9 ad un'ora prima del tramonto. Giorni festivi dalle ore 9 alle 13.

BATHS OF CARACALLA. - Via delle Terme di Caracalla.
9 a.m. till an hour before sunset. Holidays 9 a.m. 1 p.m.

THERMES DE CARACALLA. - Via delle Terme di Caracalla.
De 9h. à 1h. avant le coucher du soleil. Jours fériés de 9h. à 13h.

THERMEN DES CARACALLA. - Via delle Terme di Caracalla.
Von 9 Uhr bis eine Stunde vor Sonnenuntergang. An Feiertagen von 9 bis 13 Uhr.

TESORO DI S. PIETRO. - Basilica di San Pietro.
Dalle ore 9 ad un'ora e 30 minuti prima dell'Ave Maria.

TREASURE OF ST. PIETRO. - Basilica of St. Peter's.
9 a.m. till an hour and 30 minutes before the « Ave Maria ».

TRESOR DE ST. PIERRE. - Basilique de St. Pierre.
De 8h. à une heure et demi avant l'Angélus du soir.

SCHATZKAMMER VON ST. PETER. - Basilika von St. Peter.
Von 9 Uhr bis eine Stunde 30 Min. vor dem Ave Maria.

TOMBA DI CECILIA METELLA. - Via Appia Antica.
Dalle ore 9 ad un'ora prima del tramonto. Il lunedì chiusa.

TOMB OF CECILIA METELLA. - Via Appia Antica.
9 a.m. till an hour before sunset. Closed on Mondays.

TOMBEAU DE CAECILIA METELLA. - Via Appia Antica.
De 9h. à une heure avant le coucher du soleil. Fermé le lundi.

GRAB DER CECILIA METELLA. - Via Appia Antica.
Von 9 Uhr bis eine Stunde vor Sonnenuntergang. Montags geschlossen.